CU00600990

Who is this
Jesus
who was
born of Mary?

Stephen Dawes

British Library Cataloguing-in-Publication Data
A catalogue record for this book is available from the British Library

ISBN 978-0-9561909-0-1

Published by Truro Cathedral Limited
Cathedral Office, 14 St Mary's Street, Truro, TR1 2AF

Printed by Mid Cornwall Printing
Unit 5, Higher Newham Lane, Newham, Truro, TR1 2ST

Contents

Introduction

Three gospels and three different ways of looking at the birth of Jesus

The New Testament begins with four gospels. They tell one story and they are about one central character, but they are written from four different perspectives. Each begins in a different way and each one tells the story differently.

Mark, the earliest of the gospels, tells us what it is about in its opening verse. It is about 'the good news of Jesus Christ, the Son of God'. Straight away Mark introduces us to the central character in the story, Jesus, and tells us that he is the 'Messiah'. Mark does this by using two messianic titles, 'Christ' (the Greek form of the Hebrew word 'Messiah') and 'Son of God', though not every translation includes 'the Son of God' because that phrase is absent from some old and important manuscripts. After that briefest of introductions Mark begins his testimony to Jesus the Messiah with the story of John the Baptist preaching in the desert, and baptizing people, including Jesus, in the River Jordan.

By contrast there are two chapters in Matthew's gospel before the account of Jesus' baptism by John; mostly they describe 'the Christmas story'. There are also two longer chapters in Luke's gospel before the scene on the banks of the Jordan, describing more of the familiar Christmas story and adding the incident in the Temple when Jesus was 12. The gospel of John does not begin with a Christmas story of any kind, but it does weave powerful teaching about Jesus and his birth into its 18-verse introduction to its version of the meeting between John the Baptist and Jesus. In this little book we will look at the opening of these three gospels and ask the question 'Who is this Jesus who was born of Mary?'

Before we go any further, here is a quiz. To do it you must read through Matthew's story of the birth of Jesus in Matthew chapters 1 and 2.

1. Where were Joseph and Mary six months before the baby was born?
2. Where were they six months after the baby was born?
3. In what kind of building was the baby born?
4. How many wise men were there?

5. What religion did the wise men practise?

6. How many times is Jesus called 'Messiah' in these chapters?

7. What other titles are given to Jesus here?

8. What nationality and/or religion was King Herod?

9. How many angel visions were there and to whom?

10. What particular feature occurs five times in these two chapters?

11. Does anything strike you in particular in reading these two chapters?

And here are the answers from Matthew's story:

1. Six months before the baby was born Joseph and Mary were in Bethlehem.

2. Six months after the baby was born they were either in Egypt or still in Bethlehem, depending on what you make of that 'two years' in 2.16.

3. When the wise men arrived the baby was in a house, and either he was born in that house or his parents moved him into it before the wise men arrived, and so here's that 'two years' question again.

4. Matthew does not say how many wise men there were.

5. Matthew does not say what religion the wise men practised, but the word he used – 'magi' – suggests they could well be Zoroastrians.

6. Jesus is called 'Messiah' four or possibly five times in these chapters (1.1, 1.16, 1.17, 1.18 and indirectly at 2.4).

7. Other titles which are given to Jesus are 'Son of David/Son of Abraham' (1.2), 'Emmanuel' (1.23), 'King of the Jews' (2.2) and indirectly 'Saviour' (1.21), 'Son of God' (2.16) and 'Shepherd' (2.7). All these, as we shall see later, are titles given to the old kings of the House of David.

8. King Herod was a Jew.

9. There were four angel visions, and it was Joseph who saw each one (1.20, 2.13, 2.19 and implied in 2.22).

10. The feature which occurs five times in these two chapters is the use of a quotation from a prophet (1.22, 2.6–7, 2.15, 2.17, 2.23).

11. I wonder if the very low profile of Mary in Matthew's story struck you at all?

And now here's another quiz. This time you must read through Luke's story of the birth of Jesus in Luke chapters 1 and 2.

1. To whom is the Gospel addressed?
2. When is the child to be born of Mary first mentioned?
3. Which Old Testament stories does chapter 1 remind you of?
4. How many angel visions were there and to whom?
5. Where were Joseph and Mary six months before the baby was born?
6. Where were they six months after the baby was born?
7. In what kind of building was the baby born?
8. Who visited the baby?
9. What titles are given to Jesus here?
10. Is there a particularly prominent one?
11. How many times is the 'Holy Spirit' mentioned?
12. What particular feature occurs three times in this section?

And here are the answers from Luke's story:

1. The gospel is addressed to Theophilus.
2. It is not clear when the child to be born of Mary is first mentioned, is it at 1.17 or 1.31?
3. The stories in Luke 1 might have reminded you of the Old Testament stories of the birth of Isaac to Sarah (Genesis 15–21), of Samuel to Hannah (1 Samuel 1) and of Samson to Manoah's wife (Judges 13).
4. There were three angel visions: one each to Zechariah (1.11), Mary (1.26) and the shepherds (2.9).
5. Six months before the baby was born Joseph and Mary were in Nazareth.
6. Six months after the baby was born Joseph and Mary were back in Nazareth.
7. The baby was born in a stable – or at least a place with a manger.
8. Shepherds visited the baby.
9. The following titles are given to Jesus: 'Son of the Most High/Son of God': 1.32, 35; 'Lord': 1.17(?), 1.44, 1.76, 2.11; 'Saviour' 1.69, 2.11, 2.30 and 'Messiah' 2.11, 2.26.

10. The title 'Saviour' seems to be the prominent one.

11. The 'Holy Spirit' is mentioned five times (1.15, 35, 41, 67, 2.25).

12. The particular feature which occurs three times in this section is the singing of songs: the *Magnificat* (1:46–55), the *Benedictus* (1:68–79), and the *Nunc Dimittis* (2:29–32).

There is no quiz on John 1, and in gratitude for that you might like to look back at the questions and answers on Matthew and Luke and see where the birth stories differ in the two of them.

Now think about what happens in your church nativity play, or what features in a crib scene or on some religious Christmas cards. Something strange has happened to the two different stories over the centuries. The two stories in Matthew and Luke have been merged into one. The result is the Christmas story of a traditional nativity play. Bethlehem. A stable. The baby in a manger. Mary sits. Joseph stands. Shepherds kneel. Three kings offer gifts. Ox and ass look on. A star. Angels. Most of that picture, though not all, comes from Matthew and Luke, but in the process of putting it together parts of Matthew's and Luke's stories have been lost. In fact, one of the things we never do at Christmas is to look carefully at what Matthew or Luke tell in their own stories. If we did, we would see that the nativity play or the composite Christmas card is simply not there. In these things bits of each story are used while other parts of both are left out. That's the only way that the two different, and sometimes conflicting, stories can be harmonized, and in doing that their distinctive testimonies to Jesus are lost.

Matthew begins with a genealogy. He traces the line of Abraham, the father of the Jewish people, down to King David and then to Jesus. He wants to demonstrate that Jesus is 'the Messiah, the son of David, the son of Abraham'. Then he tells how this Messiah was born. In the reign of King Herod of Judea (who died in 4 BC) an angel appears to Joseph telling him that his fiancée is pregnant and that this pregnancy is the work of God. Joseph still marries her and the baby is born at home in Bethlehem. Wise men follow a star and bring gifts but ask Herod the way. He seeks the baby for different reasons and when he can't find him kills all the young boys in the area. Joseph and Mary flee to Egypt as refugees. They stay there until Herod dies and then try to go home to

Bethlehem. Finding a son of Herod on the throne they decide to go to Galilee, a separate country, and settle in the village of Nazareth instead. God is at work here to save God's people: but it is a tragic story. The Messiah is born but his own people do not accept him. Foreign wise men, priests of an eastern religion, worship him but Herod and the wise men and priests of Jerusalem reject him. Matthew's story of the rest of Jesus' life will unfold in the same way, and his biography will end with Jesus telling his disciples to 'go out into all the world'.

Luke's birth story is quite different. It starts with the birth of Jesus' cousin, John the Baptist, to Elizabeth, a barren woman. Luke expects his readers to know, from stories in the Old Testament, that God is always at work in such births. The angel Gabriel appears to Mary, who lives in Nazareth, announces her own imminent pregnancy and tells her about Elizabeth's. Mary visits her. Mary and Joseph get engaged. They have to journey to Bethlehem for a Roman census. Jesus is born in a stable there because the inn is full. Shepherds visit. After eight days Jesus is circumcised and four weeks later Mary and Joseph take him to the Temple in Jerusalem to offer the proper thanksgiving. Then they go home to Nazareth. All the people in Luke's story are ordinary; none are rich, powerful or important. That is the way Jesus' life will unfold in this gospel. He will live among such people and care especially for the despised and the outcast. Luke also has a genealogy, and in it he traces Jesus back past David and Abraham to Adam, to show that Jesus is for all humanity.

In the chapters that follow we shall look carefully at Matthew's birth stories, then at Luke's and then at the Prologue to John's gospel. In doing so we will try to take the stories as told very seriously, and we will deliberately try not to harmonize them into a neat fit. We will work on the assumption, however, that hard facts about the first Christmas are few, namely that Jesus was born and that his mother was Mary; and that we don't know when, or where or anything at all about the circumstances surrounding the birth. That might worry some people, but it needn't. It obviously didn't worry the first Christian thinker, Paul; or the first gospel writer, Mark, for that's all they said on the subject. You can ask 'Is it true?' and 'Did it really happen like that?' even though our quiz results have pointed out those places where if Matthew's story is true, then Luke's must be false, and vice versa, but asking those kinds of questions about much in the Bible never really gets us very far. A far better question to ask is 'What do these stories mean?'

Just before we start, another question is important. Why did the gospel writers tell such stories in the first place? The answer is that the Christmas stories were a celebration. In story, drama, poetry and song the first Christians celebrated the impact Jesus of Nazareth had on them, on how they thought, on their values, attitudes and lifestyles. They didn't, at that stage, produce creeds or work out definitions of who and what Jesus was; the doctrine of the Trinity and similar issues came much later. Instead they sang songs and told stories because that was the way their Jewish culture traditionally expressed its deepest convictions about the meaning of life, the universe and everything. So we shall keep the two stories in Matthew and Luke separate in order to see their distinctive testimonies to Jesus; and then we shall look at how John does it differently still. Our quest in each case is to look at their answers to the question, 'Who is this Jesus who was born of Mary?'

Questions for reflection

1. Have you noticed the differences between the two stories in Matthew and Luke before?

2. How important do you think the 'Is it true?' and 'Did it really Happen like that?' questions are?

3. Do you find it surprising that there is no 'Christmas message' in the writings of Paul, the great missionary evangelist, or in Mark's gospel? Why do you think this is?

1   Matthew chapter 1

If you read through the first two chapters of Matthew again, you will see that they can be divided into seven sections:

1	1.1	the first verse
2	1.2–17	the 'birth-record' or genealogy
3	1.18–25	the annunciation to Joseph
4	2.1–12	the visit of the wise men
5	2.13–15	the escape to Egypt
6	2.16–18	the slaughter of the innocents
7	2.19–23	the migration to Nazareth.

Before we look at the first three of these in this chapter I invite you to stop reading, pick up a pen, have a think and complete this sentence: 'According to Matthew, this Jesus who was born of Mary is . . . ' And you must promise not to turn to the end of chapter 2 to see what my suggestion is!

Before we go on there is one more question. You have just identified, in the sentence you have completed, the main theme, or plot or storyline in Matthew's Christmas story. Do you think there is any noticeable minor theme or secondary plot or storyline? And you must promise not to turn to the end of chapter 2 to see what my suggestion here is either!

Matthew 1.1: The first verse

The opening verse of Matthew is not such a bold title verse as that of Mark, but it does three things. First, it tells us that the book is about 'Jesus'. Second, it tells us who and what he is, 'Jesus the Messiah'. Third, it introduces the genealogy or 'birth record' of Jesus by identifying him as 'the son of David, the son of Abraham'. By the end of the verse we are in no doubt about the huge claim Matthew is making about Jesus.

There is another interesting comparison between the opening verses of Matthew and Mark too, at least in the *New Revised Standard Version* (NRSV). The two Greek words 'Jesus' and 'Christ' are exactly the same in both gospels, but for some reason the NRSV translates them as 'Jesus Christ' in Mark and 'Jesus the Messiah' in Matthew. Both translations are correct, because the Greek term 'Christ' and the Hebrew one 'Messiah' mean the same thing ('Anointed One' would be the English translation), but it is odd that the NRSV should translate them differently; no other major translation does it. Personally, I prefer 'Jesus the Messiah' or even 'Messiah Jesus' to 'Jesus Christ' because it reminds us that 'Jesus' was his name and that the other word was originally the title the first Christians gave him, whereas 'Jesus Christ' just sounds like two names. Matthew is claiming a lot when he gives Jesus the title of 'Messiah' or 'Christ' at the beginning of his book, and we will return to this important title later.

Matthew 1.2–17: The 'birth-record' or genealogy

I can guarantee that these verses are rarely read in carol services. They remind us of those odd and boring bits of the Old Testament where 'Zebad begat Ephial and Ephial begat . . .' and so on until the reader loses the will to live. Although these verses may seem dull to us, by using a genealogy Matthew is able to stake his claim for Jesus and prove its worth right at the beginning of his gospel, at least for his first readers who understood the codes and conventions of genealogies.

Genealogies in the Old Testament were used to prove legitimacy, to demonstrate that someone had the right to do what they did. For example, the genealogy in 1 Chronicles 6.31–53 establishes who could and could not serve as priests and Levites. Genealogies also gave shape and structure to the past, to show where the present fitted in or where a particular story started; for example, the genealogy in Genesis 5 is used to set the scene for the story of Noah. Both these ideas are used here. By tracing the ancestry of Jesus to David, Israel's greatest king, who was called God's 'Messiah' (or 'Christ' or 'Anointed One'), Matthew establishes Jesus' credentials as his legitimate heir, the new 'Messiah', God's present Anointed One, the true 'Son of David'. And by tracing his ancestry to Abraham, and in so doing retelling the story of the history of the 'children of Abraham', Matthew shows that the life of Jesus is the next chapter in the story of God's dealing with both Israel and the world, which began with the call of Abraham and God's promises to him (Genesis 12.1–3).

The conclusion of the list in verse 17 contains another significant feature: numbers. It points out that this genealogy is in three equal parts, with 14 generations from Abraham to David, 14 from David to the Exile, and 14 from the Exile to Jesus, though if you count the first and last of these they contain 14 names each but only 13 actual generations! There are similar discrepancies in Matthew's maths if you check his genealogy against some of those in the Old Testament; for example, in 1 Chronicles 3.10–14 there are three more names between Solomon and Jechoniah. If we ask why Matthew has three sets of 14 each, we get much ingenuity but no very satisfactory answers. Perhaps the best is that the numerical value of the name 'David' is 14? It may be that this kind of coded maths lies behind Paul's statement in Galatians 4.4 that, 'When the fullness of time had come, God sent his Son, born . . . ' which is his only reference to the birth of Jesus, for what is clear from this sequence in Matthew 1 is Matthew's belief that Jesus is the final part of a plan.

Although biblical genealogies don't have the accuracy sought by people trying to trace their ancestors (if you are still not convinced you can see that some of the details in Luke's genealogy of Jesus differ from Matthew's), there is an interesting, and quite possibly crucially important, detail in Matthew's birth-record of Jesus here. It is that he mentions four mothers, in addition to Mary at the end. At least two, and possibly all of them, are foreign. In verse 5 we find Rahab, usually understood to be the Canaanite prostitute from Jericho (Joshua 2.1–21, 6.22–25) although this doesn't quite fit the dates; and Ruth the Moabite (Ruth 4.13–22) as great-grandmother, and grandmother of David. The other two mothers are Tamar in verse 3, the widow who seduced her father-in-law Judah (Genesis 38.6–30) and in verse 6, Bathsheba, though she isn't named, the victim of rape by David himself (2 Samuel 11). If they were all foreigners this might explain Matthew's mention of them, for he is interested in 'foreigners and the gospel', as we shall see. It is more likely, however, that he includes them because there was something 'irregular', even scandalous, about their marriages, as there certainly was, for Matthew, with the marriage of Joseph and Mary with which his genealogy ends.

No details of the life-stories of any of the four women is given in the genealogy, just as nothing is said about any of the men. It could be that Matthew assumes that his readers would know that Abraham was only the father of Isaac after quite a struggle and then only by the grace of God in extreme old age; that Jacob was not Isaac's real heir but a cheat who robbed his brother of his birthright and his blessing; that Judah was not all he should have been; that Solomon and his mother had to plot hard for him to become David's successor; that Solomon's son Rehoboam was a nightmare as king; that the prophet Elijah regarded King Ahaz as a disaster and his son Manasseh even worse. So Matthew's version of Jesus' birth-record includes some unsavoury characters and incidents of which no one could be very proud. It also shows the general downhill slide of Abraham's descendants after the time of David, when the rot which set in with Solomon ended in the dreadful deportation to Babylon. And after the return from Babylon almost every name belongs to a nonentity. The time is indeed ripe for a Messiah.

And Messiah comes. His name is Jesus. His father is Joseph. His mother is Mary. When it mentions the other four mothers, the genealogy gives first the name of the father, then that of the son, and finally that of the mother 'by whom' the father had fathered the child. Matthew does not use that formula in verse 16, however, about Joseph, Jesus and Mary. He puts it quite differently, referring to 'Joseph, the husband of Mary, of whom Jesus was born'. This is the first sign in Matthew's gospel that there might be something odd about the birth of Jesus, odder even than the births to the four women he has mentioned, or than the birth of Isaac.

Matthew 1.18–25: The annunciation to Joseph

This is about how odd the birth of Jesus was and why he was born at all.

In verse 18, in case it has passed us by, Matthew tells us for the fourth time that he is writing about the Messiah, and that Jesus is that Messiah. Here, he says, he will tell us the circumstances of his birth. And the circumstances he recounts are unusual, to say the least. Mary and Joseph are 'engaged', that is, legally contracted to marry but not yet married. Mary finds herself pregnant. Joseph decides to end the engagement. An angel explains to him what is going on. Joseph marries Mary immediately. In due course the baby is born and named.

Before we come to the theology here, verse 19 poses a slight difficulty. There is no problem with the reference to Joseph as Mary's 'husband' or Mary as Joseph's 'wife' even though they are not yet fully married. In that culture 'betrothal' was the first part of a two-stage marriage process and constituted a binding contract which enabled the couple to be thought of as husband and wife. The second part was when the husband took the wife into his house and they began to live together. Joseph and Mary were at stage one. The problem lies in what is said about Joseph. He has two options when faced with Mary's pregnancy. The first is to go for stage two immediately, to take her into his home and hope that no one counts the dates too carefully when the baby is born, just as, we may imagine, many another couple had to do. The other is to 'dismiss' her, that is, to end the betrothal/marriage and 'divorce' her; which would also be a way of telling the world that he was not guilty of illicit sex when Mary's pregnancy became obvious. Verse 19 says that he intends to take the second option, but to do it quietly so that Mary is not exposed to public shame. That, of course, would be impossible for time would inevitably expose her as the mother of an illegitimate child and Joseph's previous breaking off of the engagement would indicate that the child was not his. That would make her situation very serious if anyone were to enforce the legal punishment for adultery. It doesn't look as if Matthew has thought through verse 19 very well.

Much more important, however, is Matthew's theology in this passage. He expresses it in four ways: in the two references to 'the Holy Spirit', in the appearance of the 'angel of the Lord', in the two names and their meanings, and in the quotation from the Old Testament.

Matthew tells us, twice, that Mary's baby is 'from the Holy Spirit' (1.18, 20). In trying to unpack this we must put out of our minds straight away the picture of the 'Holy Spirit' as the 'third person of the Trinity' for that concept belongs several hundred years in the future from the time when Matthew was writing, and in any case he would have found it incomprehensible as well as unnecessary. In the Old Testament, which would have been Matthew's theological encyclopaedia and dictionary, there are no references to 'the Holy Spirit' with a capital H and a capital S, and only three to God's 'holy spirit' which he has put into or given to someone (Psalm 51.11; Isaiah 63.10, 11). But there are plenty of references to God's 'spirit' or 'the spirit of God' or 'the spirit of the LORD', and especially to this spirit 'coming upon' prophets and ancient heroes and equipping them for the task God wanted them to do (e.g. 1 Samuel 11.6, 16.13; 2 Chronicles 15.1, 20.14 and frequently in Judges, e.g. 3.10, 6.34, 11.29, 13.25, 14.6, 14.19, 15.14). These all have the same meaning. To speak about God's 'spirit' was an established way of speaking about the power of God. So it is here in Matthew. Mary is pregnant because God's power has 'come upon' her and made her so. Mary's pregnancy is part of God's planning, God's power and work.

It is therefore no surprise that an angel enters the story at this point. Just as Judges talks frequently about God's spirit coming upon people, so also it contains a number of angel appearances (2.1–5, 5.23, 6.11–24, 13.3–23). In the Old Testament angels are usually members of the 'heavenly host' sent to deliver a message, though they can be human messengers as well. As this one appears in a dream, it looks like one of the first variety. Interestingly, angels appear in the stories about the miraculous birth of Isaac to the aged Sarah and Abraham (Genesis 18.1–8, 19.1–3, Hebrews 13.2) and in the birth of the hero Samson to the barren wife of Manoah (Judges 13.3–23). The appearance of an angel confirms that all this is the work of God, and the angel's dream message to Joseph makes this explicit.

The angel addresses Joseph as 'Son of David', reminding us for the third time of Jesus' Davidic lineage. He explains that Mary's pregnancy is a work of God, and gives the child a name, 'Jesus'. This is the later version of the old Hebrew name 'Joshua', which means 'God saves', and it is given because 'saving his people' is what this child will do (1.21). At the end of the angel's message Matthew adds his own explanation of Mary's pregnancy which ends in a second name for the child. He will be called 'Emmanuel', because the child will be 'God with us'. Given the importance of names and naming in both the Old Testament and the New this is a crucial step in Matthew's storytelling.

Finally, in verses 22–23 we come to a unique, characteristic and very important feature of Matthew's birth story. He has already, in several different ways, made the point that the birth of Jesus is part of God's plan and work. Here he makes that explicit by using a quotation from the Old Testament introduced by a formula which talks about the fulfilment of prophecy. He will do it another four times: at 2.5–6, 2.15, 2.17–18 and 2.23. This is such an important feature of these chapters, and one so frequently misunderstood, that we must have a separate look at Matthew's purpose. It is plain enough: he uses this and all his quotes to demonstrate that Jesus is the climax of God's long-term plan to save

God's people. As for the 'Virgin Birth' detail, we'll leave that for now and consider it in chapter 3 when we look at Luke's use of the same idea.

Matthew's use of quotations from 'prophecy'

What is Matthew's purpose in quoting Isaiah 7.14 and other Old Testament verses in these two chapters? Is it to suggest that Isaiah 7.14 predicts the virgin birth of Jesus, or that Hosea 11.1 predicts the Holy Family's time as refugees in Egypt? This is an important issue, which we will work through in stages, concentrating on Matthew's use of Isaiah 7.14 in 1.22–23.

Isaiah 7.1–17, in comparison with some passages from the prophets in the Old Testament, is very straightforward. The historical situation to which it refers is clear and can be dated to around 734 BC. The nations of Syria and Israel (Ephraim) have come together in a coalition against the rising power of Assyria and they want little Judah to join in. King Ahaz of Judah is thrown into a panic about what to do. Isaiah goes to him with a message from God about his predicament – 'Don't worry about that futile coalition. Ignore it and it will go away. Trust in God! If you don't, he will give you something far more terrible to worry about than these two tiny neighbours: the full might of Assyria itself!'

In a lovely bit of drama laced with sarcasm Isaiah tells the king not to worry about Israel and Syria, as God will deal with them. 'What are you worrying about them for?' he asks. 'Syria is no more than Damascus its capital! Worried about Damascus? It's no more than Rezin its king! Worried about Rezin? He's nothing more than a smouldering stump of a firebrand! You think you are facing a great fire –it's just a bit of charred and smouldering stick!' Then Isaiah invites Ahaz to ask for a sign from God, and we see Ahaz the religious hypocrite. Until now he hasn't had any faith in God at all and suddenly he comes out with the pious 'Far be it from me to ask the Lord for a sign', as the old translation put it. Isaiah is obviously thoroughly irritated by this point, and replies that he's getting a sign whether he likes it or not.

The sign is the birth and infancy of a child. The meaning is plain, that by the time a woman can conceive, have her baby and the child grow old enough to tell right from wrong the threat from Pekah and Rezin will be past. Most recent translations say 'young woman'; only two have 'virgin' (*New International Version* and *New King James Version*). A *Good News Bible* footnote puts the explanation succinctly, saying that the Hebrew word used here is not the specific word for a virgin but for any young woman of marriageable age. The use of 'virgin' comes from the Greek translation (the 'Septuagint') made 500 years later, and is influenced by Matthew's use of that word, and by the Christian doctrine of the Virgin Birth.

Commentators make a variety of suggestions about which young woman Isaiah is talking about: one of the king's wives, or possibly the prophet's own wife. We know that Isaiah gave his children peculiar names in order to reinforce his message (7.3, 8.3) and the name 'Immanuel' would be appropriate for a prophet's son as a sign of a new message. It is more likely, however, that the woman in question was one of King Ahaz's wives, and that the name could be a 'throne name', given to a royal child at birth (like the names in Isaiah 9.6, also read at Christmas), for the child is mentioned again in 8.8 where he appears to have grown up to be king. Apart from these few questions there is no difficulty with Isaiah 7. As a piece of prophetic narrative it is as straightforward as any you will find. It has a clear meaning in its historical context and, providing you ask the important questions about when and where, that meaning is easily understood.

The problem arises when we turn to Matthew 1.22–23 where Matthew takes up Isaiah 7.14 and uses it in a very different way when he says that this sign is 'fulfilled' in the birth of Jesus to the virgin Mary. Matthew's translation is close to that of the Septuagint, the early Greek translation, though none of his quotations are exact ones and both translate the more general Hebrew word in Isaiah with the specific Greek word for 'virgin'. Matthew seems to say, and this is certainly how the verse is traditionally understood, that Isaiah was predicting the birth of Jesus.

He says much the same thing in his other quotations. All of them, except 2.5 quoting Micah 5.2, are said to be 'fulfilled' in the events surrounding Jesus' birth. In 2.5 in answer to the wise men's questions about where they can find the newborn king, the scribes quote Micah 5.2 about Bethlehem. When Joseph and Mary flee as refugees into Egypt (2.14–15), this is said 'to fulfil what had been spoken by the Lord through the prophet', and Hosea 11.1 is quoted, which originally referred to the people of Israel coming out of Egypt in the Exodus. In 2.17 the massacre of the innocents is said to fulfil 'what had been spoken through the prophet Jeremiah', and Matthew quotes the wailing in Ramah which in Jeremiah 31.15 refers to the distress that accompanied the exile. Mary and Joseph's eventual return from Egypt in 2.23 and their setting up home in Nazareth (where according to Matthew they had never lived before, of course) is said to be in fulfilment of 'that which had been spoken through the prophets'. Here Matthew quotes a little verse which causes a problem because we can't find it in the Old Testament at all. There are references in the Old Testament to people being called 'Nazirites', but they are concerned with taking a vow. Presumably somebody living in Nazareth would have been called a 'Nazarethite'. Where Matthew got 'Nazorean' from remains a mystery. These sort of 'prophecy-fulfilled' quotations continue through the gospel, but they are really concentrated here in the birth story.

What is Matthew doing? Obviously he is using the Old Testament in a very particular way for his own purposes. Of all the quotations in Matthew 1–2 the only one that is legitimate by our standards is the one from Micah, because it actually mentions the coming of the Messiah, how and when and where that will be. None of the other quotations which he uses are 'messianic' in their original setting. None of them are predictions of the coming of the Messiah in the future. We have been taught to read the prophets in their original settings and take those historical settings seriously. We have been encouraged, in fact, to read any verse in its context, and to take that context seriously. If we do that with the five verses Matthew quotes, however, we see that only one of them has any reference to the Messiah. So what are we to make of Matthew's use of the Old Testament?

I want to assume that Matthew is neither a fool nor a charlatan, though we could, of course, dismiss him as either or both of these. We could say that he has no sense of the meaning of the Old Testament, and that he has put in his thumb and pulled out the plum he wanted; or that he believed that all prophecy was about predicting the future, therefore every prophetic word could be read as a prediction. We could say that he was quite deliberately finding texts that would prove his point and lifting them straight out of their context in order to make them do just that. We all do that at times, and as a way of using the Bible the method

17

has a long history and a certain legitimacy. But I want to suggest that Matthew's purpose is far more subtle and much more deserving of our careful attention, and I want to illustrate this from the Emmanuel text. At one level, as we have seen, Matthew's use of this text from Isaiah is not legitimate. The plain, obvious and straightforward meaning of Isaiah 7.14 is the same one that Isaiah gave to King Ahaz. In his reply to the king's panic in 734 BC it was no use at all for Isaiah to tell him not to worry because the Messiah is coming in 740 years' time! Isaiah's prophecy, the same as most Old Testament prophecy, is not that sort of prediction. At another level, however, I suggest that Matthew's use of Isaiah 7.14 is both legitimate and thought-provoking.

Why were the words of the prophets preserved at all? Why were the words of particular people in quite specific times and places collected and preserved for posterity? Why were the words of a particular prophet called Isaiah, to a particular king called Ahaz, at a particular time in 734 BC, about a particular historical situation remembered, saved, passed on and eventually written down? The answer appears to be that these words were preserved because they were thought to be useful for the future, because they spoke of what God had done in a particular setting in the past. They were heard as a message that God had given in a particular place, which would enable people in similar times and places in the future to understand what the requirements or promises of God might be for them. They were a record, or example, of the way God dealt with his people in a particular situation and since God was the God of yesterday, today and tomorrow, the record of the past was obviously a guide to how God might be expected to act now or in the future. So the words of the prophets were preserved in order that people could gain inspiration from, or be warned by past events or experiences. Later generations could look back and read such words and be encouraged or warned by them. Old stories had lessons for new situations. This is exactly what we do when we read the Bible in worship and preach sermons about texts, incidents, people or experiences from it.

We know from the Dead Sea Scrolls that, at the time of Jesus, the words of the old prophets who had spoken to their times and places in the name of God were reused in this way. For example, an important find at Qumran is a commentary on the book of the prophet Habakkuk. Time and again the commentator updates Habakkuk's words. Habakkuk said a lot about the 'wicked' oppressing the 'righteous', a common theme in the message of the prophets, but when the Qumran commentator reaches the first of Habakkuk's references (Habakkuk 1.4), he says, 'Interpreted, "the wicked" is the Wicked Prince and "the righteous" is the Teacher of Righteousness', the latter being the head of the Qumran community and the former the High Priest in Jerusalem! It is clear from this that by the time of Jesus old texts were believed to have multiple meanings or multiple applications, the original, plus contemporary ones. And we continue to treat the Bible like this ourselves. We take, for example, a word of Amos in the eighth century BC about the rich trampling the poor (eg Amos 5.11) and say that this is about fair trade today. We do not for one moment imagine that Amos is predicting our 21st century economy: but we do think that his ancient words have current applications. They did the same at Qumran, and so did Matthew.

Matthew knew that in its original setting the Emmanuel oracle was about salvation, about God's deliverance of King Ahaz and the people of Judah from Pekah and Rezin. Isaiah promised through this oracle and sign that Ahaz and Jerusalem would be delivered, and they were. The Syro-Ephraimite coalition was destroyed by Assyria, and Ahaz sat safely in Jerusalem while it took place. So the oracle and sign 'worked': God delivered Ahaz and Jerusalem as he said he would. That, presumably, is why someone somewhere decided that Isaiah's words should be remembered and written down for posterity. So Matthew uses this ancient salvation story to make the point that a greater and fuller salvation is now here, that the Jesus whose birth he is recounting is the true deliverer and the bringer of full salvation. He is not saying that Isaiah's words *predicted* Jesus but he is saying that Jesus *fulfils* Isaiah's words, an important distinction. He wants us to understand that, although God's deliverance of Jerusalem at the time of Ahaz was real, now in Jesus Christ we have something that makes that pale into insignificance. In this sense Jesus is indeed the 'fulfilment' of Jerusalem's salvation, the real Emmanuel.

If this is Matthew's logic, then it solves the problem of the use of Isaiah 7.14 in Matthew 1.23, and all the rest of Matthew's Old Testament quotes in the birth stories as well. It also helps to clear up the persistent misunderstanding that prophecy in the Old Testament is about prediction of the future. When Matthew says that the coming of Jesus fulfils these words of Isaiah he is not saying that Isaiah predicted Jesus. We might read it like that, but I hope that I have said enough to suggest that that is not the way that it should be read, for if that is what Isaiah really did then his ministry to Ahaz was nonsense. When we read in Matthew 1.23 that the birth of Jesus to the virgin Mary took place 'to fulfil what the Lord had spoken by the prophet', we read it best if we see the point that whatever happened with Isaiah and Ahaz, though real enough, is just a foretaste of the salvation and deliverance which is now present in Jesus.

Questions for reflection

1   What do you make of the scandalous women in the genealogy?

2   'Biblical prophecy is forth-telling not fore-telling' is how it is sometimes put. What do you think?

3   'Christology' is the technical term for 'teaching about' or 'doctrine of' Christ, i.e. who Jesus is and what he does. What do you consider, at this stage, are the main features of Matthew's Christology?

2   Matthew chapter 2

Matthew 2.1-12: The visit of the wise men

This chapter opens with the visit of the wise men, the 'magi'. The word seems to have been used first for priests of Media (modern Iran) in the sixth century BC who were skilled in the art of interpreting dreams, then for Zoroastrian priests, and then for serious astrologers. But when we read of 'magi' at the Persian court in Daniel 1.20 it is clear that the writer of that book doesn't think much of them. Other ancient writers, too, regarded them as magicians, charlatans or, worse, as those who were engaged in the occult. Acts portrays two magi very negatively (Simon in Acts 8.9-13 and Elymas in Acts 13.6). There is, however, nothing negative in the way Matthew portrays them, and it is probable that the magi in his narrative came from the more respectable end of the spectrum.

We are not told how quickly after the birth these exotic visitors arrived. In our nativity plays they kneel before the manger in which the new-born child is laid. In the classic western Christian calendar they arrive at Epiphany, when the baby is 12 days old: but in Matthew's account there is no indication of time. In verse 16 King Herod attempts to kill all the children in the area under two years of age, which might suggest that by the time the wise men arrived Jesus was a toddler, getting under Mary's feet as she did the housework in their house in Bethlehem. For, just as there is no indication that the wise men arrived immediately after the baby's birth, so there is no manger, no stable and no journey down from Nazareth in Matthew. His story so far indicates that Jesus was born at home, in Bethlehem.

There are two big themes in this section. The first is the status and identity of the baby, and here Bethlehem is an important pointer. It is the place where King David had been born, and it would be the place where his true successor would be born too, as the wise men were told by the experts at the palace in Jerusalem. They had come seeking the 'child who has been born king of the Jews' (their words). Herod asks his experts where the 'Messiah' (his word) is to be born. This point is reinforced in the second of Matthew's 'prophecy-fulfilled' sayings, as verse 6 quotes from Micah 5.2. Here the experts quote ancient words which do indeed look forward to the coming of a new king/messiah and the dawn of a new age. Matthew's version of the saying is different from those in both the Greek Old Testament and the Hebrew Bible, which say that Bethlehem is, despite its famous son, a pretty small and insignificant place! Matthew's version gives it a bit of a boost. He also adds an extra bit to the quote which he takes from 2 Samuel 5.2, words with which King David himself had been commissioned as 'shepherd' of all God's people. Matthew's message cannot be plainer: Jesus is the Messiah, the King of the Jews. It is he for whom the wise men were looking (v.2), whom they find (v.11), and whom Herod will seek to destroy (v.16). Their gifts, many commentators point out, are gifts fit for a king.

The second big theme is that of who welcomes Jesus the Messiah and who does not, and what this means. Even if they are reputable magi, these wise men are from the east; they are foreigners, Gentiles, non-Jews. But they have travelled long to find this baby, and when they see him, they kneel and pay him homage. King Herod 'and all Jerusalem with him' are the opposite. They are Jews, the people of the promise and the covenant, the chosen ones. But when they hear about their king, they try to find him in order to kill him. The Fourth gospel doesn't tell this story, but in its introduction to the life and ministry of Jesus it makes precisely the same point, 'He came to what was his own, and his own people did not accept him' (John 1.11). At this point we might also think of the ending of Matthew's gospel: the risen Jesus acknowledges that 'all authority in heaven and on earth' has been given to him, and sends his Jewish disciples out to 'make disciples of all nations' (Matthew 28.18–19). Everything has been turned around. From the very beginning of his life to the end of his ministry on the cross, the King of the Jews had been rejected by his own people. At the beginning of his life a few foreigners had travelled to him and knelt before his infant authority, and at its end his disciples were to travel into all the world to share what those first magi had seen and believed. This is an important point in Matthew's storytelling, but there is something else too. One of the hopes for the Messiah's coming was that the Gentiles would come to Jerusalem looking for God, offering their homage and bringing their gifts (e.g. Isaiah 2.2-4, Micah 4.1-2). In Matthew's story, that is exactly what happens. The magi come from the east, offer their homage and bring their gifts. It all adds up to a bold statement that the New Age has dawned.

And so to the gifts. The traditional interpretation of the three gifts has been gold for Jesus as king, frankincense for Jesus as God, and myrrh for Jesus as dying Saviour, and there is much to reflect on in that way of looking at them. However, there may be more. There are some interesting foreign visitors in the Old Testament. One is the magus Balaam in Numbers 32–34 who comes from the east and blesses Israel. Another is the Queen of Sheba who comes from the south and brings gifts to King Solomon in 1 Kings 10.1–10. Some commentators see these characters lurking here and suggest that Matthew's storytelling is deliberately alluding to them in Psalm 72.10–11, 15 and to the gifts of gold and frankincense in Isaiah 60.1–6. He does not quote from these passages, they suggest, but he draws them into the picture he is painting of Jesus as the King of the Jews. These two passages, incidentally, might also explain why, by the end of the second century, the 'magi' began to be called 'Kings'.

This brings us to the star. Every Christmas, guaranteed, there is a newspaper article about the star, as some astronomer or another thinks they have identified which star it was, or who thinks they have discovered something new. There are a number of traditional theories: it was a supernova, a star which explodes with great brightness for a month or two; it was a comet, even the famous Halley's Comet which appeared in 12 BC; it was a planetary conjunction, maybe a particularly spectacular conjunction of Jupiter and Saturn, which did happen three times in 7 BC. But we might be looking in entirely the wrong place – after all, how can a star stop over a particular house? We have already seen how Matthew builds up his story by reference after reference to the Old Testament, by direct quotes, by allusions and by Old Testament devices like his genealogy. It is, arguably, the same with this star. Forget astronomy. Look up the words of that magus Balaam in Numbers 24.17 for example, and add to it Isaiah 60.1–3 (and note how this is part of the same passage that mentions gold and frankincense). Then add one more thing; that the doomed leader of the second Jewish revolt against the Romans in AD 130 was called Simon bar Cochba ('Simon son of the Star'), which showed that these verses had messianic overtones for the Jews of the day just as Revelation 22.16 did for the early Christians. On the other hand, of course, Matthew's readers would have found nothing odd in the idea of a heavenly portent announcing the birth of a great person; anyone who was anyone – such as Alexander the Great and

Caesar Augustus – had had one. Likewise they would be familiar with the idea that such portents announced a great event (e.g. Josephus, the great Jewish historian, tells of a star over Jerusalem prior to its destruction by the Romans in the first Jewish Revolt in AD 70). Matthew would have been familiar with this way of looking at things. He might also have known that Halley's Comet, or whatever it was, had been seen sometime thereabouts, and so used it in his story. The end result is the same. The star is there to point to the tremendous significance of Jesus.

However you regard this story – that it is totally historically accurate, or that it is a piece of glorious theological fiction or something in between (and we will come back to that question after we have looked at the birth stories in Luke) – its message is unmistakable: Jesus is the Messiah, the King of the Jews, in whose birth the New Age has dawned.

Matthew 2.13–15: The escape to Egypt

In one sense this short passage is simply the continuation of the story of the Holy Family, the wise men and King Herod. The hint of danger and our suspicion of King Herod, aroused in verses 3 and 8, are now seen to be real. The child is at deadly risk, and here we have first sight of the vulnerability of this life which will be cut short in death on a cross. The wise men, warned in a dream, go back east, but not via Jerusalem. Joseph, also warned in a dream, leaves home and goes south with Mary and her child. They go to Egypt, a significant place in the Bible story. Egypt was the place of slavery, of the brickyards where the family's ancestors had been forced to work (Exodus 1.5). Every year at Passover the Jews remembered how God had rescued them through Moses, and gave thanks to the God who had 'brought them out of the land of Egypt, out of the house of slavery' (Exodus 20.2). But it had not always been like that, for the Patriarchs had found refuge there from famine and crisis generations before Moses, and centuries later Jeremiah and many more would find safety there as refugees when the Babylonians destroyed Jerusalem. As a result there was now a very large Jewish community in Egypt, including several hundred thousand in the great city of Alexandria. So, in the story in Matthew, Joseph and Mary join the 'Jews of the Dispersion' and settle in Egypt for an unspecified length of time, until the death of Herod, which happened in our dating in 4 BC.

None of this happens by accident, Matthew reminds us with another quote from his Bible; it is all part of God's plan. This time he quotes from Hosea 11.1 which refers to God bringing his son (the Israelite nation) out of Egypt in the great Exodus led by Moses. In using this quotation is Matthew also hinting at the great new beginning in Israel's life which is happening now? God had called his old 'son' out of Egypt back then, but that son had grown up and failed to mature into the flourishing adult that God had intended. Now he is bringing a new Son out of Egypt! The story continues, but as before, there is more to it than appears at first.

Matthew 2.16-18: The slaughter of the innocents

In one sense this is the tragic ending of the story of the Holy Family, the wise men and King Herod. The Holy Family are safely away. So are the wise men. Herod massacres the children under two years in the area of Bethlehem, to make sure that he has killed the one he thinks might pose a threat to his rule. If this really happened, and it is quite in keeping with what we know of Herod and his family's methods, it is tragic. But Josephus, writing only 50 years later, doesn't mention it, and he usually doesn't miss a chance to portray Herod and his family in the worst possible light. It could simply be, of course, that 'all the little boys he killed at Bethlem in his fury' only amounted to a negligible few dozen, a mere jotting in the margin of history's volumes on the violence and cheapness of human life.

Here too we have another quote, a sure sign that Matthew wants us to see something more than another minor human tragedy. He quotes Jeremiah 31.15, words which form part of a chapter of hope and promise, that the people of the old southern kingdom of Judah, whom the Babylonians have recently exiled (following the fall of Jerusalem in 586 BC) will soon go home and be fully and gloriously blessed. In verse 15 Jeremiah addresses 'Ramah', a village in which he and other captives on the way to Babylon had been temporarily held and from which he himself had been released (Jeremiah 40.1). It had been part of the old northern kingdom of Israel whose people had been exiled by the Assyrians two centuries before (following the fall of Samaria in 722 BC). Jeremiah's message was that the Israelites would be rescued and return home too, just like the Judeans. Rachel, wife of the patriarch Jacob and ancestress of the northern tribes who was buried near Bethlehem, will be comforted, assured Jeremiah. Matthew does not quote the reassuring part of this story, only the tragic part, and it may be that in doing so he intends to show that even this tragedy – the slaughter of the little boys of Bethlehem – is part of God's plan and therefore it is not entirely meaningless. It may be that we ought to read this quotation alert to the fact that it offers hope in this tragedy, and does not only voice despair. It was widely felt at the time of Jesus that Israel was, in fact, still in exile: in her own land, oppressed by the occupying Romans and exiled from the freedom intended for God's people. And this feeling intensified after the failure of the Jewish revolt and the destruction of the Temple in AD 70. Matthew and his first readers could well identify with Rachel's wailing, just as they would yearn for the fulfilment of the promise that came next in the passage from Jeremiah. Matthew is doing more here than telling a tragic story – he is offering a glorious hope.

Matthew 2.19–23: The migration to Nazareth

After Herod's death the family moves on. Another angel message tells Joseph that it is safe to 'go to the land of Israel' and he sets out for home, obviously intending to return to Bethlehem. But when he gets near and hears that one of Herod's sons is ruling Judea, he continues north, after another dream warning, and settles in Nazareth, even though the province of Galilee was ruled by another son of Herod, though Matthew doesn't mention that. This is the first mention of Nazareth in Matthew, and in Matthew's story Joseph comes to Nazareth as an outsider and 'settles there like an incomer', which is the meaning of the Greek verb he uses and which NRSV translates as 'made his home in'.

We have already seen that the quote he uses about this is odd, for we can't find anything exactly like it in the Old Testament. He may have made a mistake, or he could be quoting from a version of an Old Testament passage which was current in his day but which has appeared in a different form in the final version of the Scriptures we have today. It could also be a play on words; some commentators think it is a reference to Isaiah 11.1, part of Isaiah's hope for a new king. There that new king is spoken of as a 'branch' (*nezer* in Hebrew) growing out of the 'stump of Jesse' (Jesse was King David's father), a reference to a coming and better king. The mystery remains. But, Matthew insists, God's purposes have been fulfilled; the angel messages have been successfully heard and acted upon, and the child has reached the place where he needs to be. Here the birth story ends. The next chapter begins some 30 years later.

The birth of Jesus in Matthew and what this tells us about him

At the beginning of chapter 1 I invited you to complete this sentence, 'According to Matthew, this Jesus who was born of Mary is . . . '. Now I would like you to look at what you wrote then, and see if you would like to change it in any way in the light of what you have read since then, without reading on beyond the end of this sentence.

Now I invite you to compare your sentence with mine: 'According to Matthew, this Jesus who was born of Mary is the long-promised Messiah of the Jewish people, that is, their king and their saviour.'

I also invited you to ask yourself if there is any noticeable minor theme or secondary plot in Matthew's storyline, and if so, what it might be. You might like to look at what you wrote then, and see if you would like to make any changes, without reading on beyond the end of this sentence.

Now I invite you to compare what you wrote with this: 'Yes: that he was despised and rejected by the Jews and welcomed by Gentiles.'

All that we have done in these chapters is to read, closely and carefully, the Christmas story found in Matthew's gospel. In so doing we have observed that it differs in detail quite significantly from the Christmas story found in Luke and that repeated in nativity plays. We have tried to explore some of the details but it is clear that there is still plenty of room for even more exploration. We have noted, and struggled with, Matthew's 'proof from prophecy' method. These difficulties apart, however, we have been able to identify both the main storyline and the secondary one with which Matthew has chosen to begin his gospel, that Jesus who was born of Mary is the long-promised Messiah of the Jewish people, their king and their saviour who from the beginning was despised and rejected by his own people and welcomed by Gentiles.

What we have not done, however, is to say what it means to call Jesus the 'Messiah'. What did Matthew and those who used this title for Jesus mean by it? What were they saying about him when they called him

'Messiah' or, in Greek, 'Christ'? However, we are not going to answer that question yet. We must put it on hold until we have looked at the birth story in Luke.

Questions for reflection

1   What do you think about my statements of Matthew's main theme and his secondary one?

2   Have you any further thoughts on what you said in answer to question 2 in the Introduction?

3   We have come to the end of Matthew's birth story. Has anything I have said about it disturbed you? Has anything excited you?

3   Luke chapter 1

If you read through the first two chapters of Luke again you will see that the birth story there can be divided into ten sections:

1	1.1-4	the introduction
2	1.5-25	Zechariah and Elizabeth
3	1.26-38	the annunciation to Mary
4	1.39-45	Mary and Elizabeth
5	1.46-56	the *Magnificat*
6	1.57-80	the birth of John the Baptist
7	2.1-7	the birth of Jesus
8	2.8-20	the visit of the shepherds
9	2.21	the circumcision of Jesus
10	2.22-39	the visit to Jerusalem.

Following this there are another 13 verses in chapter 2: verse 40 is a note about Jesus growing up, verses 41–51 tell us about a visit to the Temple when Jesus is 12 years old and verse 52 is another note on his progress. Whether verse 40 belongs with verses 22–39 or with verses 41–51 is an editorial decision. As there are no paragraphs in the old manuscripts we'll consider 2.39 to be the end of Luke's birth story.

As we did with Matthew, before we look at the first five of these sections in this chapter I invite you to stop reading, pick up a pen, have a think and complete this sentence: 'According to Luke, this Jesus who was born of Mary is . . . '. And you must promise not to turn to the end of chapter 4 to see what my suggestion is!

Again, there is another question. You have identified the main theme or plot or storyline in Luke's Christmas story in the sentence you have just completed. Do you think there is any noticeable minor theme, secondary plot or storyline? And you must promise not to turn to the end of chapter 4 to see what my suggestion here is either!

Luke 1.1–4: The introduction

The interpretation of this introduction has often supported the idea that of all the gospels Luke's is the most historically accurate, and even that

Luke can properly be described as a 'historian'. We have already seen that there are differences between Matthew's and Luke's birth stories, the most obvious one being the Holy Family's destination after the baby's birth. Did they flee to Egypt and then eventually settle as incomers in Nazareth, or did they wander home to Nazareth via Jerusalem and carry on much as before? Those who feel that there must be more factual bedrock in these stories than the two facts I work with (that Jesus was born, and that his mother's name was Mary) will take some comfort from Luke's introduction here, and will already give him some benefit of the doubt over Matthew. He dedicates his book to 'Theophilus', who might be a real high-ranking Roman Christian somewhere, or the dedication might be to any Christian reader who is 'loved by God', which is the meaning of the name. He promises his reader an 'orderly account' and given that he is using Mark as one of his sources one wonders if he is suggesting that Mark's account is disorderly, or improperly researched or even both? Whatever his feeling about Mark's writing, he does make it clear that he himself writes as one Christian believer to another, and that his purpose is to clarify and explain more about those things which Theophilus has already been taught. Like other writers of ancient historical works, he intends to give instruction – in this case theological instruction – and in the manner of a classic historian he begins by saying that he has researched his material well, not least by listening carefully to the original eye-witnesses and preachers ('servants of the word'). Unlike Mark and Matthew there is no mention yet of Jesus, but there is a very loaded word in the first sentence. Luke will write, he says, of 'the events that have been *fulfilled* among us', and in that word 'fulfilled' we can see that Luke, like Matthew, sees the birth of Jesus as the culmination of the story of the Old Testament, and as the story of God's purposes and plan.

Luke 1.5–25: Zechariah and Elizabeth

Luke's story begins gently and proceeds slowly. It opens with a note setting the scene in 'the days of King Herod of Judea', who ruled over Judea from his fortress palace in Jerusalem from 37-4 BC according to our calendar. In contrast to that public figure, the next two characters mentioned are very ordinary – a minor priest and his wife. They are good people, but something is wrong. The priest's wife, Elizabeth, is barren and the couple are getting older. This is a big clue, for Luke's original hearers or readers, as to where the story is heading. The appearance of a barren woman in several Old Testament stories means that God is about to do something significant. Think of Sarah, Rebekah, Manoah's wife and Hannah. God had promised Abraham many descendants, but he was old and Sarah was barren. The story of how the two of them lost patience with God, tried to engineer things their own way, made a mess of it, and how eventually she conceived Isaac is told in Genesis 16-21. Isaac and Rebekah's similar problem is described in Genesis 25. There's quite a gap after that until the story of Manoah's wife in Judges 13. Here again things are bad: Abraham's descendents are now numerous enough to be divided into 12 tribes who are in the process of settling into the Promised Land (the second promise God had made to Abraham), but the local inhabitants are troublesome and the Israelites are having a hard time. It's time for God to act again, and he does; this anonymous barren woman – Manoah's wife – gives birth to the great, though morally dubious, hero Samson. Shortly after that God gives his people a better gift, the last and greatest of the 'judges', the prophet and king-maker, Samuel. He is the son of another barren woman, Hannah, whose story we read in 1 Samuel 1-2. So as soon as you read that Elizabeth is old and barren, you know that something important is going to happen, to do with God's plans to help his people.

So the story unfolds. Zechariah is going about his business, and has been chosen by lot, as was the custom of the priesthood, to offer incense. While he is doing so, an angel appears: major clue number two. As we saw in chapter 1, the presence of angels means that God is at work. And so Zechariah is told just what God is doing: first, he will arrange for Elizabeth to have a son, and second, that son will have a role to play in the major events that will take place later. The instructions about no wine or strong drink in verse 15 are the same as those given to Manoah's wife in Judges 13; and Hannah abstains from the same in 1 Samuel 1. Both their children are named as 'nazirites' – men dedicated to God; and although that title is not given to Elizabeth's boy, he is clearly expected to be dedicated to his special task. God will empower him in a special way. He will be filled with 'the Holy Spirit', Luke's way of speaking about God's power. He will be Elijah, or like Elijah, preparing the people for God. Verse 17 quotes Malachi 4.5-6 where this idea of the return of the prophet Elijah (who had not died but who had been taken up into heaven - 2 Kings 2) before the 'Day of the Lord' is first found (see also

Sirach/Ecclesiasticus 48.10 in the Apocrypha). Many commentators see a reference to the Messiah and to Jesus in the 'him' of verse 17, and so speak of John as the 'forerunner to the Messiah'. This is why I gave two answers to question 2 about Luke in the Introduction. As I see it, however, there is no mention here of the Messiah; John will go before God, preparing for the coming 'Day of the Lord', the time when God's kingdom will come and his will be done on earth as it is in heaven.

Like Abraham, Zechariah is not entirely convinced, and so he is given his own sign – he is struck dumb – as both a confirmation of what will happen and a warning that it is unwise to disbelieve an angel. And this is no ordinary angel: this is Gabriel, who appears in the Old Testament as a divine messenger 'having the appearance of a man' sent to tell Daniel what is about to happen and what his visions mean (Daniel 8.16, 9.21). When his tour of duty in the temple is over Zechariah goes home, though where he lives in Judah we are not told. Elizabeth conceives, and for some unknown reason remains in seclusion for five months; she reveals her pregnancy in month six. In doing so she bears testimony that 'this is what God has done'.

Luke 1.26–38: The annunciation to Mary

The scene shifts to Nazareth in Galilee, six months later. In Matthew it was Joseph who received three or probably four dream visions involving an angel; in Luke he receives none. Instead Mary is visited by Gabriel who tells her about her impending pregnancy and about the baby himself. The baby is named, though unlike Matthew's account, there is no explanation of the name's meaning. Instead the angel spells out that the baby will be great; that he will be called, 'the Son of the Most High God'; that he will be given David's throne; and that he will reign over Israel for ever. This adds up to the fact that Jesus will be the Messiah. Mary is, naturally, confused. Before anything happened she was introduced twice as a virgin (v.27) and now, after being told about the pregnancy, she points out the difficulty to Gabriel that she hasn't had sex with anyone yet (v.34). Using two different expressions Gabriel points out that this baby is God's responsibility (v.35), and, to reinforce the point that nothing is impossible with God, he cites the pregnancy of Mary's older, barren, cousin Elizabeth. Then in a verse which has been the text of countless sermons, Mary offers herself to God to use as God sees fit. Everything connected with the birth of Jesus is God's work, the story insists.

The 'Virgin Birth'

We saw in chapter 1 that Matthew uses the words of Isaiah 7.14 as a further part of his argument that Jesus is the culmination of God's great plan to 'save' his people. Traditional Christian teaching, however, has seen more than that in this quotation and has used it as an important part of the foundation of the doctrine of the 'Virgin Birth', supported by what the angel has already said in Matthew 1.20 and what will be said in 1.25. This idea is boosted considerably by the longer story of the annunciation to Mary in Luke 1.26–38. Strictly speaking all these passages talk about a 'virginal conception' rather than a 'virgin birth', but we'll stick with 'virgin birth' as the usual shorthand. Whilst the rest of the New Testament is silent on the topic, there can be no denying that the birth stories in both Matthew and Luke say that Mary conceived her baby without any human fathering.

The New Testament does not support, however, any of the later doctrines which grew up about Mary, such as that of the 'Immaculate Conception', which teaches that from the moment of her conception she was free from 'original sin'; or that of her 'Perpetual Virginity', i.e. that she remained a virgin after Jesus' birth. The plain meaning of Mark 3.31–35 and Acts 1.14 is that Mary went on to become the mother of other children who were Jesus' brothers and sisters. The argument that these were Jesus' step-brothers and step-sisters, Joseph's children by a former wife, has nothing to support it. Equally, there is nothing in the concept of a virgin birth in Matthew and Luke, or anywhere else in the New Testament, to support later ideas about the nature of Christ as 'fully God' and 'fully man' and how it was possible for him to be both of these at the same time. This was an important discussion in the Church three centuries later, but there is no sign of it on Matthew's agenda, or in Luke's annunciation story.

Matthew and Luke do express, however, in slightly different ways and without any interest in gynaecological or biological detail, an insistence that God was at work in the birth of Jesus. We will see in chapter 6 that John says the same. The old stories had shown that, to achieve God's purposes, God could make barren wombs fruitful, and the new story about Elizabeth says the same. The story about Mary shows us that God can do the same with a virgin's womb, too.

In our quiz in the Introduction we saw that the 'Holy Spirit' is mentioned five times in Luke's birth story, in addition to Matthew's two references which we looked at in chapter 1. The term is used in Luke in exactly the same way as it is in Matthew. The first reference to the 'Holy Spirit' (I would prefer not to use capital letters, but I will follow the convention in NRSV) at Luke 1.15 refers to the adult John the Baptist being empowered by God, as the great heroes of old had been. The third and fourth references are in 1.41 and 1.67, where, in typical Old Testament style Elizabeth and then Zechariah are each empowered with a prophetic message. The same is true of Simeon in Luke 2.25. Putting them all together like this shows that the remaining reference, at 1.35, suggests that it is the same power of God which will conceive the promised baby in the virgin Mary's womb. Or at least I take that to be the obvious implication of this verse, as do most commentators. The alternative interpretation is that the baby Mary will soon conceive naturally will then be supernaturally empowered by God, thus removing any sense of a virgin birth from Luke at all. That seems just a tad too easy so, opting for the first interpretation, I think this verse uses two terms for God's power (the 'Holy Spirit' and the 'power of the Most High') which will bring about the child's conception.

Finally, we need to remember here that in this ancient Jewish culture virginity was not a condition to be prized or praised, but was something to be lost as soon as possible by getting married and having children. Those few women who did not marry were to be pitied, as were those who did not have children, for theirs was a sorry, unnatural and unblessed state of emptiness and poverty. A vestige of this poor opinion of virginity remains in the verse in the *Te Deum* that 'When thou tookest upon thee to deliver man, thou didst not abhor the virgin's womb' which is watered down in the more recent version to 'when you took our flesh to set us free you humbly chose the virgin's womb'. The idea of virginity as the best and most blessed state for women was a much later development in a particular church at a particular time. So the virgin birth story is at one with other stories of God opening wombs and making them fruitful, and in each case it is the outcome which matters, the child who is born. So here, the emphasis in Matthew's virgin quote and in Luke's annunciation story is not on Mary, nor on how she conceived or gave birth, but on the child she bore and the place of that child in God's purposes.

We can't be certain who were the intended readers or hearers of these two gospels. Traditionally Matthew has been thought of as writing primarily for a Jewish-Christian audience and Luke primarily for Gentile-Christians, and there is much to commend that view. At the same time it is clear enough that when these two gospels were written, probably sometime in the AD 80s, most Christian communities had both Jewish and Gentile members. The Jewish membership of the Church would have recognized the allusions to which we have referred, and have been familiar with the old stories; and would, presumably, have found Matthew and Luke's arguments and stories compelling. It is possible that Gentile members of the churches might have found things easier: for just as in their folklore the births of great heroes were accompanied by portents in the sky and in nature, so too Greek folklore and mythology had its share of children fathered by various gods. One hopes, however, that they had learned that the One True God did not behave in such ways.

Luke 1.39–45: Mary and Elizabeth

Mary hurries to visit Elizabeth and Elizabeth's six-month foetus moves in her womb. Throughout this gospel John the Baptist will be presented as recognizing that Jesus is the Messiah, and that he himself is the Messiah's Forerunner. The same is true of the way the relationship between them is portrayed in the other three gospels. Reading between the lines, however, historians suggest that there may have been tensions and possible rivalries between the two men's supporters and followers. From the beginning, Luke's story says, however, that John has known his place and rejoiced in it.

Notice carefully how this meeting begins. Mary enters the house and greets Elizabeth. That is all. Everything that Elizabeth then says is given to her by the Holy Spirit, as she is empowered by God's Spirit with the gift of insight and authority. So Elizabeth blesses Mary twice and the child she will bear once; Elizabeth recognizes who Mary is ('the mother of my Lord') and who the baby will be ('my Lord'). And so Elizabeth knows what the Lord had said to Mary via Gabriel. What she says is important too: a prayer that Mary and the baby will be blessed by God, and a statement affirming that they are blessed by God. Again there are Old Testament precedents for this form of blessing (Judges 5.24 and, from the Apocrypha, Judith 13.18), and its content (Deuteronomy 28.4). Elizabeth's words will be taken up later in the gospel at Luke 11.27–28.

Here also we have two uses of the term 'Lord', the first referring to Jesus, and the second to God. The word had a whole range of meanings in both Jewish and Greek culture: a woman might refer to her husband as 'my Lord'; a tenant would certainly refer to their landlord in that way, as would a plaintiff to a judge, and ordinary people to those in authority or people higher in the social hierarchies which existed at the time. Above all was the Roman Emperor, and 'Lord' was one of the usual titles which signified his total supremacy. To call anyone else 'Lord' in that sense amounted to conspiracy and rebellion. At the same time in prayer, worship and teaching the Jews used the term for their God and, for some of them at least, doing so was a deliberately subversive act. There is only one Lord, no matter what the Emperor might want to call himself! Here, however, is the first unambiguous use of the term with reference to Jesus in Luke's story, and at the very least it confirms the authority which Jesus is to have.

Luke 1.46–56: The *Magnificat*

Mary's song of praise, the *Magnificat* (the title is from the Latin of its third word, 'magnifies') has featured in Christian worship in many ways over many centuries and still does. Recently it has been much taken up by Liberation and Feminist theologians because of its radical teaching about power and God's bias to the poor and marginalized. Some versions of the Bible add a footnote to 'And Mary said' in verse 46 to say that there are a few ancient manuscripts which point to Elizabeth, and not Mary, as the singer of this song. Some commentators also note that this fits better with the contents of the song itself, as the old and barren Elizabeth was more marginalized than the young Mary, and that the song is more appropriate on the lips of an old woman now blessed with a baby. Be that as it may, Luke borrowed the theme and some of the words from the Song of Hannah which that previously barren woman sang when she handed over her son, Samuel, to a life dedicated to God in the temple at Shiloh (1 Samuel 2.1–10).

We saw in chapter 1 that Matthew makes links with the Old Testament through quotations. Luke does the same with this song he puts on the lips of Mary (or possibly Elizabeth) and the two other songs he uses, sung by Zechariah (the *Benedictus* in 1.68–79) and by Simeon (the *Nunc Dimittis* in 2:29–32). In doing this he draws on the great songs in the Old Testament which celebrate what God has done. These vary from relatively small-scale thanksgivings, like Hannah's or the Song of Deborah in Judges 5 (one of the oldest passages in the Old Testament), to major ones like the Songs of Moses and Miriam in thanksgiving for the escape from Egypt in Exodus 15; the two Songs of Moses at the end of his life and on the verge of the Promised Land in Deuteronomy 32 and 33; and the Song of Habakkuk in Habakkuk 3 which itself echoes these. These songs are scattered through the Old Testament, and to them must be added, of course, the songs of praise to God gathered together in the Book of Psalms. By inserting these songs Luke uses a traditional method of giving praise to God for what he has done and is doing, and he also makes sure that the life of Jesus is seen in terms of the ongoing action of God. Here, he says, is the next chapter in the old, old story!

The *Magnificat* is a patchwork of phrases and themes from the Old Testament and the Apocrypha reproduced in the style of an Individual-Praise psalm and using the traditional Hebrew form of poetic parallelism, which involves balancing or repeating the sense of the first line in the second one. In case you want to check the references, they are:

verse 47	1 Samuel 2.1-2, Psalm 35.9, Habakkuk 3.18
verse 48	Genesis 29.32 and 30.13, 1 Samuel 1.11, Psalm 31.7, 2 Esdras 9.45
verse 49	Deuteronomy 10.21, Psalm 111.9, Zephaniah 3.17
verse 50	Psalm 103.17, Psalms of Solomon 13.11
verse 51	Psalms 89.10 and 118.15
verses 52-53	1 Samuel 2.7-8, Job 5.11 and 12.19, Psalms 89.10 and 107.9, Ezekiel 21.26, Sirach 10.14
verse 54	Psalm 98.3, Isaiah 41.8, Psalms of Solomon 10.4
verse 55	2 Samuel 22.51, Micah 7.20.

The structure of the Song is simple. It opens with Mary's testimony that God is great and that his greatness is to be both recognized and rejoiced in. This declaration names God in two different ways, as 'Lord' (the third use of that term in three verses) and as 'Saviour'. In our second quiz in the Introduction we identified both these terms as titles applied to Jesus in Luke's birth stories, with 'Saviour' being perhaps the most prominent. In the light of that, the use of these two titles for God here builds up Luke's picture of the uniqueness and importance of Jesus as God's agent. After this introduction the Song gives example after example of God's saving work in generously raising up some and putting down others. Those whom God lifts up are, like Mary (and Elizabeth), those who 'revere' him (a much better translation of the Greek word and the Hebrew one which lies behind it than 'fear'), the 'lowly' and the 'hungry'. Those whom God puts down are the 'proud', the 'powerful' and the 'rich'. This language is straight out of the Book of Psalms, where these contrasting terms are used for the 'righteous' and the 'wicked' respectively, i.e. those who take God seriously and try to do what God requires, and those who don't. And, just as in the Psalms, these terms are not meant to be taken just figuratively or metaphorically. It was obvious to some of the psalmists, as it had been to the prophets and as it would be to John the Baptist and to Jesus, that power and wealth can and do corrupt, and that pride is a sign of that corruption. Though it would be simplistic to draw the opposite conclusion, that the poor are always humble or that poverty leads to spirituality, there is certainly a strand in Luke's thinking that sees the poor as blessed and the rich as cursed (see Luke 6.20–25). There were a number of Jewish groups at the time who called themselves 'the Poor', as a group of Jewish Christians would do later (the 'Ebyonim' or the 'Ebionites' – 'the Poor Ones'). By using these terms Luke sets the scene in which Jesus would live and work and indicates the future priorities of Jesus' mission. The Song ends by referring back to God's promise of blessing to Abraham and his descendants (Genesis 12.1–3), and highlights the fact that these events of Elizabeth and Mary's pregnancies are to be seen as part of the fulfilment of those ancient promises.

Luke 1.57–80: The birth of John the Baptist

Elizabeth gives birth to her baby (vv.57-58) and, to everyone's surprise he is named 'John' ('Gift of God' or 'God gave') at his circumcision (vv.59-66). To everyone's greater surprise Zechariah gets his voice back. The friends and neighbours see this as a portent and speculate about what the baby will become. It is already obvious, somehow, that the 'hand of the Lord' is upon him – another way of speaking about God's power, in parallel to the 'spirit of the Lord', for example (v.66).

The crowd's speculation is answered in Zechariah's song, the *Benedictus* (from its first word in Latin) in Luke 1.67–78. Empowered by the Holy Spirit, Zechariah speaks out and announces who this baby is and what he will be and do. The first part of his Song echoes that of Mary, and the second repeats the gist of what the angel Gabriel had told Joseph. Like Mary's song, this one too is a patchwork of quotations, themes and allusions to the Old Testament and the Apocrypha:

verse 68	the opening line is a common liturgical expression in the Old Testament, for examples see 1 Kings 1.48 and Psalms 41.13, 72.18 and 106.48; for the rest of this verse see Psalm 111.9
verse 69	(note that the Greek here has 'a horn of salvation' and the only modern English translation to have this is the *New International Version*) Judges 3.9, 1 Samuel 2.10, Psalms 8.3 and 132.16, Ezekiel 29.21
verse 70	2 Chronicles 36.22, Wisdom of Solomon 11.1
verse 71	Psalms 18.18 and 106.10
verse 72	Micah 7.20
verses 73-75	Genesis 26.3, Exodus 2.24, 1 Kings 9.4-5, Psalms 18.18, 89.4, 105.8-11 and 106.45, Isaiah 38.20, Jeremiah 11.5
verse 76	Isaiah 40.3, Malachi 3.1 and 23
verse 77	there are no scriptural allusions here – is this significant? Is this where John and Jesus will add to what has gone before?
verse 78	Numbers 24.17, Isaiah 60.1, Malachi 4.2
verse 79	Psalm 197.10, Isaiah 9.1, 42.6-7 and 59.8.

The theme of this Song is that God is now in the act of fulfilling God's promises. It assumes that God's people are in trouble; that they need to be saved (vv.69, 71), redeemed (v.68) and rescued (v.73) from their 'enemies' (vv.71 and 73). This is standard and traditional language from the Book of Psalms, but the trouble and need of which it speaks is no less real for all that. Zechariah speaks out as God's messenger with the good news that God has seen this trouble and, because of his covenant commitment to Abraham, is about to sort it out. So he announces that the age-old yearnings for a new age of peace, hope and joy, expressed by old prophet after old prophet, is now about to dawn. A new and brighter future is at hand. And so the Song moves on to speak directly to this little boy. His father tells him that he has the job of a prophet, to announce what God is doing; and of more than a prophet, to be the Elijah-forerunner, as Gabriel had told him, going before the Messiah who is the 'mighty saviour' or 'horn of salvation' of verse 69 and, not so ambiguously now, the 'Lord' of verse 76. John's particular task will be to prepare people to experience the new freedom that God is bringing them through the forgiveness of their sins (v.77).

The chapter ends with a note about the boy growing up and then being 'in the wilderness' (v.80). This is always an important place in the Old Testament. It is where God met his people as they journeyed towards the Promised Land after their escape from Egypt and, where, among other things, God made the covenant with them on Mount Sinai. It is the place of refuge to which the prophet Elijah fled in despair and then met God again (1 Kings 19). It is also the place where roads would be prepared and oases appear as they journeyed home from exile in Babylon (Isaiah 40.3-4, 43.19). This verse gives a note of expectancy and promise to Luke's story before he begins to tell of the birth of Mary's son.

Questions for reflection

1   Some churches make a lot of the 'Virgin Birth' and of the Virgin Mary. Others don't. Does it matter?

2   In this chapter I have been working on the assumption that Luke is writing creatively rather than reporting accurately. What do you think about this?

3   You will have seen that there are a lot of Old Testament quotes, allusions and echoes in Luke chapter 1. Had you noticed this before? What do you think about it?

4   Luke chapter 2

Luke 2.1–7: The birth of Jesus

Luke opened his story by setting it 'in the days of King Herod of Judea' (1.5). Here in the next instalment he sets the story in a more global context with his reference to the Emperor Augustus. The Roman Empire will feature occasionally in his gospel and will then be prominent in its sequel, Acts, which ends with the apostle Paul under house arrest in Rome but 'proclaiming the kingdom of God and teaching about the Lord Jesus Christ with all boldness and without hindrance' (Acts 28.30). Judea, Galilee, Bethlehem and Nazareth might be insignificant places, Luke suggests, but what takes place there is of international significance.

People trying to discover if these stories are historically true are faced with a problem here. Luke seems to be quite precise in dating Jesus' birth when he refers to the census taken 'while Quirinius was governor of Syria' (Syria was the Roman province which included Judea). There are records of Quirinius as governor of Syria; there are also records of a local census. However, those records date Quirinius' governorship from AD 6, and they record a census in Judea but not in Galilee, certainly not a universal one, in AD 6-7 as well. At the same time Matthew and Luke both date these events to the time of King Herod, who died in 4 BC. It is also hard to see how a Roman census could have taken place in Judea while Herod was king and Judea was still nominally independent of Rome; even though Herod was a client king he wasn't that much of a puppet! On the other hand, when Judea was finally annexed by the Romans in AD 6 when they deposed Herod's son, Archelaus, they did conduct such a census for tax purposes; it resulted in a revolt led by Judas the Galilean (who gets a mention in Acts 5.37). There have been many attempts to square this Quirinius-Herod-census circle; perhaps it is best to conclude that Luke is not the historian some would suggest.

The plain reading of Matthew's story is that Joseph and Mary lived in Bethlehem, and if we had no gospel of Luke we wouldn't give that a second thought. But in Luke's account they live in Nazareth. In both gospels, however, Jesus is born in Bethlehem. Luke needs the census to get them 75 miles south, through Samaria and across the border of Judea to 'David's city'. Matthew makes the point twice that the baby was a descendent of David (once via the genealogy and then in the way that the angel addresses Joseph as 'son of David' in 1.20). Luke highlights it too: that's why Joseph has to go to Bethlehem for the census. 'Son of David' and 'born in royal David's city' are important themes in both of these Birth Stories. Whether either story is based on fact or in history could keep us engaged for several pages. My personal view is that they are probably not, but I think also that it is much better to see both accounts as powerful statements about who and what Matthew and Luke believe Jesus to be, as testimonies to his significance and his role rather than as facts on his birth certificate. 'Bethlehem' is another way of testifying that Jesus is the Messiah.

So Jesus, Mary's first-born, is born in Bethlehem. Luke doesn't elaborate, as many Christmas sermons do, on the 'no room in the inn' theme, and the meaning of the word he uses for the place which had no room for the family is uncertain. 'Lodgings' is perhaps the best translation, just as Hannah stayed in lodgings when she visited the temple at Shiloh in 1 Samuel 1.18. It wasn't an inn like the Spotted Camel in Jericho where the Good Samaritan took the injured traveller (Luke 10.34) as that uses a different Greek word, and this is too early for synagogues with overnight hospitality suites. It perhaps means something like a 'khan' or caravanserai, where travellers slept under one roof on a slightly raised area while their animals slept at the other end of the same building. Likewise it's not certain what Luke means by manger, whether this is an animal's stall or a feeding trough. Both are possible; but we'll look again at 'manger' later in the chapter. The word does seem to be important to Luke as he mentions it three times (vv.7, 12 and 16). Luke might be saying that the sleeping end of the lodgings was full so they ended up in the animal end. At the very least he identifies Jesus as being of very humble birth, which, of course, King David was too. He might have been good-looking but he was only the eighth son of a small farmer, with hands dirty from keeping sheep (1 Samuel 16.1–13).

So we come to the 'bands of cloth' ('swaddling clothes') of verse 7. Christmas sermons often speak of these as a poor mother's way of keeping her baby warm and dressed, and that could well be all that is meant. But there is a scriptural reference to swaddling clothes, and I hope by now that I have convinced you that it's well worth looking up all of the features of the birth stories in the Scriptures that Matthew and

Luke drew upon. The reference is to the Wisdom of Solomon 7.4 in the Apocrypha, where the anonymous writer, in the name of King Solomon, says that he was 'nursed with care in swaddling cloths'. He follows that immediately with 'For no king has had a different beginning of existence' (v.5). Am I reading too much into this by suggesting that Luke's reference to swaddling clothes here is yet another pointer to the fact that Jesus is to be seen as the Messiah, the king of David's line?

Luke 2.8–20: The visit of the shepherds

Foreign magi visit in Matthew's gospel. Local shepherds visit in Luke's. What had hitherto been known only to four people is now announced publicly. Why Luke should choose shepherds to represent the general public is an impossible question to answer. Some, of course, would say that he didn't choose anyone because that is what actually happened. A popular suggestion for why Luke included shepherds is that theirs was something of a despised profession at the time, at least in the eyes of the religious leaders, because their working conditions made it almost impossible for them to keep the required rules and regulations. There is, however, no real evidence for this; and it also perpetuates a misunderstanding of the role of rules and regulations in the Jewish faith of the period. In the Old Testament, of course, shepherds have an honourable pedigree. Keeping sheep and goats was an ordinary activity and some of the greatest names in the past had been shepherds, even if some of them had prospered to the extent that they no longer got their own hands dirty. 'Shepherd' was also a term used for the kings and leaders, and even though the prophet Ezekiel had spoken out against the 'shepherds' of his day as a thoroughly bad lot (Ezekiel 34) the term was still used respectfully, as the quote from Micah in Matthew 2.6 shows. Not only that: God himself was pictured as a shepherd (Psalm 23 is the classic example) and in John's gospel Jesus is happy to refer to himself as a shepherd (John 10). And, to mention it once more, King David had been a shepherd too. The idea that the shepherds here stand for the outcasts and the marginalized among whom Jesus will live out his ministry is a modern, popular and attractive one, but it may not be what Luke had in mind. Do they simply represent the ordinary people of God?

The angel Gabriel had appeared to Zechariah and Elizabeth, and now a nameless angel appears to the shepherds who are, naturally, terrified. Its message is 'good news' ('gospel') which will bring great joy to everyone, and verse 11 spells it out in an impressive and growing crescendo: a birth, today, in David's city, a Saviour, the Messiah, the Lord! Here, as we saw in our quiz, are three of Luke's biggest words about Jesus and we shall return to them at the end of this chapter.

I used to think that verse 12, diverting the attention from the big picture to a child, swaddling clothes and a manger, was a deliberate anticlimax, alerting us to what will come in the rest of the gospel, that Jesus is not the Messiah of popular expectations but of a quite different kind altogether. Now I am not so sure, partly because of the possible 'royal' overtones of swaddling clothes which we saw above, but also because of this 'manger' which gets three mentions in this chapter. Commentators point to Isaiah 1.3, from which the ox and ass get imported into nativity scenes. The beginning of Isaiah's indictment of the failings of Israel (Isaiah 1.2–3), however, points to the scandal that while ox and ass know their owners and their master's crib/manger ('the hand that feeds them', as we might say) the people of Israel do not. With that verse in mind we can see a progression through Luke's three mentions of the manger. In verse 7 the holy baby is placed in the manger because there is no place for him anywhere else; so are things just as they always have been: God's people have no room for God and do not know him? In verse 12 the shepherds are told precisely who is in the manger, but what will they do? In verse 16 they go to the manger and tell everyone who and what the baby in the manger is! This is the opposite of what the people of Isaiah's day did; already things are different! Again, of course, you may think this is reading too much into the account. And what about the possibility that this reference to a 'child' (v.12) is alluding to Isaiah 9.6, which gets into the traditional Christmas script via Handel's *Messiah*?

The angel is joined by many more who praise God and announce the significance of this birth, that it brings God's peace and favour to all, or God's peace to favoured people (the translation problem arises because two different forms of the Greek word for 'favour/good will' are found in the ancient manuscripts). The shepherds respond to the angel's invitation, go to Bethlehem, find the manger, tell everyone what had happened to them and go back to work rejoicing. Their hearers are amazed. Mary treasures their words and 'ponders them in her heart', in the same way as old Jacob did when his son Joseph told him and his brothers about his strange dreams (Genesis 37.11). Here are things which need to be understood and interpreted; God and later events will make them clear. Verse 19 has a note of 'watch this space' about it.

Luke 2.21: The circumcision of Jesus

This verse simply records that, at the proper time, Joseph and Mary carry out Gabriel's instructions to Mary, and name the baby 'Jesus'. Strangely, neither here nor there does Luke explain that this name means 'God saves/Saviour' as Matthew had explained to his readers (1.21). By circumcision the baby takes his place among God's covenant people, the Jews. As in Matthew, Luke includes a genealogy to make this same point, but not until he has written about Jesus' baptism 30 years later (Luke 3.23–38). By circumcision and then by baptism, Luke suggests, Jesus identifies completely with God's people.

In the introduction I said that Paul has almost nothing to say about the birth of Jesus. He refers to it only once, in Galatians 4.4, where he says that 'when the right time came', God sent his Son, who was 'born of a woman' and 'born under the Law'. Luke and Matthew spell these headings out (we could have another quiz at this point – write out those four headings and then go through Matthew and Luke and note which bits of their birth stories go under which heading). Luke is very keen on the last heading, and in this note on Jesus' circumcision and the one which follows on Mary's 'purification' he takes pains to show not just that Jesus was a Jew, but that he was from the beginning an observant Jew from a family of believing and practising Jews.

Luke 2.22–39: The visit to Jerusalem

The visit to the Temple provides the opportunity for two more testimonies to Jesus, and another Song.

Two rites were necessary after the birth of a first-born son, and Luke has put them together here. One, which was needed after every birth, was that the mother should be 'purified'. According to the Old Testament regulations this was to be observed 40 days after the birth of a son and 80 after the birth of a daughter, and the mother had to go to the Temple and offer a sacrifice. Verse 24 is a quote from these regulations (Leviticus 12). The other, in the case of a first-born son, was that the baby had to be 'redeemed'. Every first-born son, the regulations said, belonged to God, and the parents had to buy him back from God with a cash payment; all of which was related to the death of the Egyptian first-born during the plagues of Egypt (Exodus 11.4–5), and in memory of the deliverance from Egypt under Moses. Verse 23 is a quote from these regulations (Exodus 13.1-16, Numbers 18.15-16). So Luke refers, mistakenly, to 'their' purification and has both Mary and Joseph visiting the Temple in Jerusalem. He also shows them as poor people, offering the cheaper form of sacrifice. We do not know how widely these regulations applied or how many new mothers actually did this in Mary's day, but Luke tells the story to portray Joseph and Mary as devout Jews.

So we come to Simeon. He is a man on whom God's Spirit 'rested' (v.25), shorthand for a prophet or some specially gifted religious person. He is guided to this couple by the Spirit (v.27), who had already told him what would happen (v.26). Three references to God's Spirit in three verses is emphasizing something and draws our attention to what he will say and do. Verse 26 prepares us for what it is, that he is about to see 'the Lord's Messiah', that is, the Messiah sent from God (the Lord). And Simeon's Song, the *Nunc Dimittis* (from its opening words in Latin) spells out what that means. He sings that God has kept his promise to him and that this baby is the one in whom God will bring about the salvation which he has promised the whole world, both Jews and Gentiles. Like the two songs in Luke 1 it weaves together texts from the Old Testament and the Apocrypha, especially from five passages in Isaiah (52.9–10, 49.6, 46.13, 42.6 and 40.5) but also Psalm 98.3, Zechariah 2.10–11 and Baruch 4.24. Particularly prominent is the material about the Gentiles, making this Song Luke's equivalent to the story of the magi in Matthew. But the Song does not say it all, there is a second speech from the old man in verses 34–35 and this introduces another nuance, just as Matthew had in his magi story. There will be salvation, peace and a glorious new beginning; but also be a turning upside-down for many, and pain for Mary.

The final scene is Anna's. She is an old and devout prophet, and as prophets do, she says what she sees. If you are looking for 'the redemption of Jerusalem', she says, then you need look no further than at this baby. The last words in Luke's birth stories lie with an old woman, possibly an old barren woman, possibly not. One word is to tell everyone what is happening; the other is to praise God for it.

In a final note about the complete faithfulness of the couple in doing everything that was required of them, Luke has them return home to Nazareth (v.39).

The birth of Jesus in Luke and what this tells us about him

In the introduction to chapter 3 I invited you to complete this sentence, 'According to Luke, this Jesus who was born of Mary is …' Now I would like you to look at what you wrote then, and see if you would like to change it in any way in the light of what you have read since, without reading on beyond the end of this sentence.

Now I invite you to compare your first sentence with mine, which is: 'According to Luke, this Jesus who was born of Mary is the Messiah, the powerful and God-given saviour of the world.'

I also invited you to ask yourself if there is any noticeable minor theme or secondary plot in Luke's storyline, and if so, what it might be. You might like to look at what you wrote and see if you would like to make any changes there too, without reading beyond the end of this sentence.

Now I invite you to compare your thoughts with mine, which are: 'Yes: that from the beginning he identifies with the marginalized.'

All that we have done in these two chapters is to read, closely and carefully, the Christmas story found in Luke's gospel. In so doing we have observed that it differs in detail quite significantly from the Christmas story found in Matthew and repeated in nativity plays. We have tried to explore some of the details but it is clear that there is still plenty of room for even more exploration. We have noted Luke's narrative introduction and his Old Testament storytelling style. We have been able to identify both the main storyline and the secondary one with which Luke has chosen to begin his gospel, that Jesus who was born of Mary is the powerful and God-given Saviour of the world, and that from the beginning he identifies with the marginalized.

Messiah

Matthew and Luke tell different stories, but the plot is the same in each of them. God is, at long last, doing something to help his people. He is bringing their 'exile' to an end. He is about to solve all the problems they experience. He is bringing 'this age' to a close. God's new dawn is breaking. Although they portray this in different ways, this is the theme of the story in both these gospels. In them the leading actor is God. God is the one who has done all the planning and controls the action, so Matthew insists with his Old Testament quotations, and Luke with his dramatic updating of famous Old Testament stories. God is the one who is doing this new thing, both of them assert through their stories of angel messengers and, above all, their talk of the 'Holy Spirit' in all of this. And God is carrying this out through this Jesus who was born of Mary. This baby is, for both Matthew and Luke, the one God will use to bring about the New Age. For both of them Jesus stands last, and greatest, in a long line of heroes whom God has used in the past; and to express that they use one title in particular for this very special child of God's planning: 'Messiah' or, in the Greek of the New Testament, 'Christ'.

Christians are prone to make two mistakes when thinking about the 'Messiah'. One is to think that all the Jews of Galilee and Judea at the time of Jesus were eagerly awaiting the coming of the Messiah. The other is to think of that Messiah as a heavenly figure rather than an earthly one. There is no doubt that many Jews of that period were hoping for a big change in the way things were, and the New Testament itself mentions a number of revolutionaries who tried to change things and failed. In the rather different, but no less revolutionary, community at Qumran they hoped for two Messiahs, a royal Messiah to be the new King, and a priestly Messiah to be the new High Priest. So there was certainly some 'messianic hope' among people, though we should not overestimate how much, and certainly not assume that everyone was hoping for exactly the same thing.

The root of this hope goes back a long way, and focuses on King David, neither the first, the holiest, nor the most powerful of the kings, but an iconic figure for all that. His dynasty lasted for 500 years in Judah until the Babylonians destroyed it in 586 BC. Later on, when the Jews tried to express their hopes for a better and brighter future, they did so by saying that God would raise up a new king like David who would be 'anointed by God', in the traditional way that kings, High Priests and even some prophets were. The King of David's line was 'the Lord's Anointed', for which the Hebrew word is 'Messiah' and the Greek is 'Christ'. So if you were walking along a street in Jerusalem in 800 BC and someone came running along shouting, 'The Messiah is coming! The Messiah is coming!' what would you do? You wouldn't look up in amazement expecting to see some heavenly warrior descending from the clouds; instead you would get out of the way before you got run over by the king in his chariot.

'Messiah' was a key term for the Davidic king and, in post-monarchy times, for his hoped-for successor. As such, the King, the *Lord's Anointed*, was special (for examples see 1 Samuel 24.6; the Royal Wedding Psalm, Psalm 45.7f; and the Coronation Psalm, Psalm 2.7). The King in Jerusalem was even called the 'Son of God' (2 Samuel 7.14, Psalms 89.26, 2.7 and 110.3). Psalm 45.6 and Isaiah 9.6 seem to go further still and talk of the king sharing in God's divinity. For a full picture of the theology of kingship in Jerusalem take a look at Psalm 89 and also the 'Royal Psalms', especially Psalms 132, 21 and 72. The King was special, exalted and in a unique relationship with God, but none the less human.

Kings were, in fact, all too human. Most of them failed to live up to expectations, and the Old Testament is not slow to point that out. Without doubt the list of royal faults in 1 Samuel 8.10-17 is based on what was remembered about the kings; and Deuteronomy 17.14-20 is perhaps the basic text on which the whole history, or sermon, of the kingdoms of Israel and Judah in the books of Samuel and Kings is based. It blames the end of Israel in 722 BC on the failure of their kings to honour God (2 Kings 17.7-18), and the exile of Judah in Babylon on the faults of its Davidic kings (e.g. 2 Kings 24.9). Nonetheless, something of a hope for a new David and a new future is seen in the curious ending of that history book at 2 Kings 25.27-30. And when, after the return from Exile, they look forwards, they express their hope in terms of a new Messiah in a new age, as we can see in Zechariah 6.9-14, 9.9-10 and Haggai 2.21-23. The idea is more common still in later Jewish literature.

Given that this is the background to the birth and indeed the whole life of Jesus, we need to note the way in which both Matthew and Luke use the ideas surrounding the Messiah in their birth stories. In Matthew, Jesus is identified as the Messiah twice in the opening verse of the gospel, once by the term itself and once in the phrase 'Son of David'. The title and the link with David reappear in the conclusion to the genealogy in Matthew 1.17–18. The search for the baby 'born king of the Jews' is central to Matthew's story of the wise men in Matthew 2, and Jesus as God's special 'Son' is the point of the third 'scripture-fulfilled' quote at Matthew 2.15. In Luke, the idea is found twice in Gabriel's annunciation to Mary (1.32 and 1.35) and in the promise to Simeon in Luke 2.26 – but it is in the angel's announcement to the shepherds that Luke puts it at its clearest. There, at Luke 2.11, the good news is announced that, in David's city, the Messiah has just been born; and in that key verse Luke also makes clear what this Messiah will do. He will be the nation's 'saviour', which reiterates that theme already sung by Zechariah in Luke 1.79, and which will be repeated by Simeon in Luke 2.30 and by Anna in Luke 2.38. Matthew makes the same point in 1.21. Luke 2.11 also unambiguously names this Messiah/Saviour as 'the Lord', to link with two possible identifications at Luke 1.16–17 and a personal one ('my Lord') at Luke 1.43. The other 26 occurrences of the term 'Lord' in these birth stories refer to God; and whatever else Luke might be doing here, he is setting the saving work of Jesus the Messiah in the context of the overall saving work of God (the same God which Mary has called 'God my Saviour' in Luke 1.47).

Without doubt, the key point for understanding Jesus, according to these otherwise significantly different Birth Stories in Matthew and Luke, is that Jesus is the Messiah. In each case, and in different ways, they both demonstrate that he is a rather strange sort of Messiah: in Matthew, contrary to all expectations, he is despised and rejected by the Jews and welcomed by Gentiles, and in Luke, from the beginning, he identifies with the marginalized. This strangeness will reappear throughout the rest of Matthew and Luke, just as it does throughout Mark. In these gospels Jesus will rarely, if ever, claim to be the Messiah, admit to it only to the disciples who he then swears to secrecy, and take pains to avoid any kind of popular recognition that he might be the Messiah; at least until the very end. Whether Jesus thought of himself as the Messiah or not is not the point – the point is that in their testimony to him written a generation afterwards that is how Matthew and Luke most clearly portray him in their birth stories.

Questions for reflection

1. A number of times in this chapter I have drawn attention to possible allusions to Old Testament passages. Some commentators, going into more detail, find even more than those I have noted. Do you think we are reading too much into the narrative?

2. What do you think about my statements about Luke's main and secondary themes?

3. We have come to the end of Luke's birth story. Has anything I have said about it disturbed you? Has anything excited you?

4. Does it make the subject any clearer to think that both 'Messiah' and 'Son of God' are titles for the kings of David's line in the Old Testament?

5   The Prologue to John - John 1: 1–18

Now for something completely different!

Before we look at John 1, let's take a moment to recap. The two birth stories of Matthew and Luke cannot be harmonized to tell one straight historical tale, but their answers to our question – 'Who is this Jesus who is born of Mary?' – are remarkably similar. Both suggest that Jesus is the 'Messiah' or 'Saviour' for whom many people of that day hoped and prayed. He is the latest and greatest of God's heroes, like David, Samuel and John the Baptist, only in a very different league! In the Prologue to John's gospel – the first 18 verses of chapter 1 – we will find something completely different.

I said in the Introduction that there was no quiz on John chapter 1. There wasn't there: but there is now, and here it is:

1. What is missing from John's treatment of the birth of Jesus that was present in Matthew's and Luke's accounts?
2. What is the key word in this Prologue?
3. Are there any other particularly important words?

And after you have answered these questions, here is some more work. I think, as do many people who have written commentaries on these verses, that this passage contains a main theme and two subsidiary themes, so now please look at it again and think about the following three questions:

4. Can you identify the verses which contain the main theme?
5. Can you identify the first subsidiary theme and bracket the verses where it is found?
6. Can you do the same with the second subsidiary theme?

Now, please pick up a pen, have a think and complete this sentence – 'According to John, this Jesus who was born of Mary is . . . '. We'll come back to this at the end of the chapter.

Here are the answers to those six questions:

1. There is very little, if any, 'story' in John. There are no people mentioned, other than Jesus and John the Baptist (leave the reference to Moses on one side for now), no places and no date. There is no material for a nativity play or a crib scene. Christmas cards based on this would have lots of words but no pictures.
2. The key word in the Prologue is the word 'Word'.
3. Other important words are 'life', 'light', 'glory', 'grace' and 'truth'.
4. The verses which carry the main theme are verses 1–5, 14, 16–18.
5. It is possible to identify one subsidiary theme about John the Baptist in verses 6–8 and verse 15.
6. The second subsidiary theme is about the response to Jesus in verses 9–13.

Finally, one more task before we go on. Please read through the Prologue again omitting the subsidiary themes, i.e. read verses 1–5, 14 and 16–18 only; and note down what difference, if any, this makes for you.

A problem entirely of our own making

I don't know what you make of the beginning of this Prologue, 'In the beginning was the Word, and the Word was with God, and the Word was God. He was in the beginning with God.' I must admit that these two verses don't make much sense to me. If, on the other hand, they are clear to you, then feel free to skip the next few pages.

Over the years I have, of course, listened to many explanations of these verses. I have heard repeatedly that they teach that Jesus is the 'Word of God', a way of speaking about him which we find occasionally in hymns such as Charles Wesley's 'Author of Faith, Eternal Word' and 'Jesus, the all-restoring Word', though these are hardly in the top ten of well-known hymns. We also find this way of referring to Jesus in Revelation 19.13, though that too is not a very well-known verse. As one way of speaking about Jesus among many others, I concede that this has a place, though, in my view, not a major place. But I don't think this way of thinking helps us with John 1 at all, because it depends on our understanding at the beginning, at the start of his argument, the point John wants to lead us to at the end. John certainly wants to say something very powerful and very important about Jesus at the *end* of his Prologue, but he doesn't start there at all, as we shall see.

I also know that if you are facing the congregation when this passage is read in carol services, you can see eyes glaze over at this point and you know that this reading has lost a good proportion of people. I know too from discussions in church groups that many Christians find this passage confusing and not very helpful at all, though they may be a bit reticent in saying so at first. I am not surprised. And it is not their fault. Every time a new translation of the Bible is published, I look up this passage straight away to see if the translators have been bold enough to do away with that misleading word 'Word' and give us something more helpful. I am always disappointed. Even imaginative and at times inspired paraphrases don't help. In the 1950s J.B. Phillips stuck to 'word':

> At the beginning God expressed himself. That personal expression, that word, was with God, and was God, and he existed with God from the beginning. All creation took place through him, and none took place without him . . . So the word of God became a human being and lived among us.

And so does the contemporary *Message* version from Eugene Peterson:

> The Word was first, the Word present to God, God present to the Word. The Word was God, in readiness for God from day one . . . The Word became flesh and blood.

All this makes me very cross because, as an explanation of what John wrote, the usual translations of these opening verses are unhelpful and also very wide of the mark. My point is a simple one. If you were sitting in a congregation in Ephesus around AD 90, listening to someone reading the opening verses of this Prologue you would not have had the slightest problem in understanding what John was saying; in fact, you might have mumbled to yourself that it was the sort of thing you had learned in primary school and when was he going to get to the point and tell you something new and interesting? And he'd keep you waiting too, waiting until verse 14 when what he said would have jolted you bolt upright, because what he says there was indeed new and revolutionary. By contrast, by the time *we* get to verse 14 we are so befuddled that we don't notice anything about that verse at all. And it's all because translating the key Greek word John uses as 'Word' just does not make much sense in English.

'In the beginning was the *Logos* ...'

My suggestion is that for the moment at least we forget entirely about 'In the beginning was the Word ...' and do not try to find an alternative English translation either. Instead let us simply use the Greek word John used. If we do that the opening verses read like this:

> In the beginning was the *Logos*, and the *Logos* was with God, and the *Logos* was God (or 'the *Logos* was divine'). He was in the beginning with God. All things came into being through him ...

and verse 14 reads, 'And the *Logos* became flesh and lived among us ...'

Next, we need to imagine John's congregation or audience. It would consist of two different groups of people. One, probably the smaller group by the time John was writing towards the end of the first century, were Greek-speaking Jews who had first joined the new Jewish sect of 'the Christians' and then stayed with it when the sect and its parent body parted company sometime after the ill-fated Jewish War of AD 67-70. These were, like the apostle Paul, mostly 'Jews of the Dispersion' who lived outside Palestine, spoke Greek and not Aramaic, and lived in the world of Greek ideas whilst maintaining their own distinctive Jewish Faith and culture. The other, larger group, were Gentile Christians who had come to faith in Christ through the missionary work in the Gentile world inaugurated by Paul. Whatever their particular ethnic group or language, they would know Greek, the universal language of the day, and be thoroughly at home in Greek culture, then the international culture of the day. Both these groups would know the meaning of *Logos*, and they would be thoroughly familiar with its important place in the thought-world of the day. They really would have learned it at primary school, and although different philosophical schools gave it different tweaks and nuances, the basic concept would have been known and accepted by almost all of them.

On the one hand they knew that the world in which they lived was always teetering on the edge of chaos and of meaninglessness. Many unexpected things happened from day to day and life was totally unpredictable and irrational. On the other hand they knew that there was a deep order to things, that day could be relied upon to follow night, and then night to follow day; that the seasons and the stars had an orderly pattern, and that human beings were able to think carefully and coherently about the meaning of life. One of their famous philosophers, Heraclitus of Ephesus (possibly where the gospel of John was written!), who lived from 535-475 BC, used an illustration that was often repeated. He said that you couldn't jump into the same river twice. By the time you had got out and jumped in again it was a different river. And of course it was. The water into which you had splashed the first time was now 10 feet or more downstream, caught up in different eddies and currents, and you couldn't stop it or gather it all together again. At the same time, of course, it was the same river, flowing between the same banks and with the same name, starting at the same source and ending in the same sea. Life, the universe and everything, suggested Heraclitus, was like that river: constantly changing, always in flux, never still. It was always teetering on the edge of chaos, of disorder, of falling apart. But it never did fall apart, even when huge catastrophes like floods and droughts and storms occurred, because there was a deep order which held it all together, gave it a structure and a shape and made it into a coherent whole. And what was Heraclitus' word for that deep order which held everything together, which gave human beings their distinctive place in it all as rational beings, the 'logical rationality behind the universe' about which they had begun to learn in primary school? Yes, you've guessed it: the *Logos*.

The problem which English translators of this Greek word have is, of course, that there is no English equivalent to that basic Greek philosophical 'big idea'. In Greek culture at that time there were several competing philosophical traditions, but the idea of *Logos* was more or less common to them all; but English, or western, culture doesn't think in that way. Our nearest equivalent might be that there is a common idea that 'God' holds everything together, but we can't translate *Logos* as 'God' in John 1.1-2 because if we did these verses would be gibberish. Instead, the translators look at the range of meanings that the word *logos* has in Greek – 'word', 'matter' 'thing', 'statement', 'speech', 'story', 'saying', 'history', 'subject', 'proposition', 'example', 'opinion', 'account', 'thought', 'reason', 'doctrine', 'teaching', 'cause' – choose one, and put a capital letter on it. And it doesn't really work because it fails to give any clue to the existence of that 'big idea' which, among others, Heraclitus had taught about and which was common knowledge at the time. But if you do remember that 'big idea', then although the opening verses are commonplace, you can see what a hugely challenging, powerful and dramatic statement John is building up to in verse 14 when he makes the amazing claim that 'the *Logos* became flesh and lived among us . . . '. It might be better not even to translate the word at all, to keep the Greek term Logos, and leave it to preachers and teachers to explain it. (I will offer you my feeble attempt to do something different in a moment.)

First, however, we must return to John's audience. To recap: everyone listening would know what the *Logos* was and then be challenged by that radical message in verse 14 that 'the *Logos* has become flesh', that the power behind the deep order of life itself has been born, or that the 'big idea' has appeared on earth as a human being.

In addition to that, the Jewish Christians in the congregation would immediately see the connection between the 'In the beginning' with which John opens the Prologue and that other 'In the beginning' at the opening of the Old Testament; and they would know how that first creation story in Genesis 1 works. In that powerful creation parable, in day-by-day stages, God speaks the world into being. God says, 'Let there be' and in response to that commanding word all things come into being. They would remember, too, how Psalm 33.6 puts this in shorthand form: 'By the word of the LORD the heavens were made, and all their host by the breath of his mouth.' They might even have heard their own preachers say the same thing (as in 2 Peter 3.5). They would also know the force of God's spoken word as expressed by God's prophets whose challenging 'Thus says the Lord' was a message to be heard and also a force in itself, which had the power to change things. Given all of this, these hearers of the Prologue would have had the added bonus of understanding the *Logos* as God's Spoken Word as well as the 'big idea' behind the universe.

So, back to the question of how to translate this Prologue for us in our very different day, where our familiar translations at best only give us the 'added bonus' without the 'big idea'. Here is my suggestion for a way of reading John 1.1–18 which tries to incorporate the 'big idea' and also separates the main theme from the subsidiary ones:

In the beginning was the Idea, and the Idea was God's, divine. It was God's Idea in the very beginning. Everything came to be because of it. Nothing came into being without it. What came to be out of it was life, life which is light in everyone. This light shines in the darkness, and the darkness never overcomes it.

A man called John was sent from God. He came as a witness to speak for light, so that everyone might have faith in God. He wasn't light itself, but he came to speak for light, saying that light itself, the light which lights everything, was coming into the world.

Light came into the world, the world which light had brought to birth, but the world did not recognize it. It came to its own, but its own did not accept it. But to all who welcomed him, who believed him, he gave power to become God's children, conceived and born from God, not naturally.

So the Idea became flesh and lived among us. We have seen his indescribable beauty, unique, full of amazing love and authentic truth. *(This was the one John saw, and who he spoke about!)* We have received from his abundance, love upon amazing love. The great gift of God's guidance was given to us through Moses, and now his amazing love and unsurpassed truth have come in Jesus Christ.

No one has ever seen God. God's only Son, the one closest of all to the Father's heart, he has made him known.

You could also try reading it again with 'Energy' instead of 'Idea'.

I would like to ask you to pause at this point, ask yourself if this helps at all, think about what works in my new translation and what doesn't, and consider if it might make a tiny bit more sense of *Logos* than the traditional versions do. I think it helps, but then I would!

Jesus is the '*Logos* incarnate'

I have suggested above that verse 14 is a crucial part of this Prologue because of its amazing claim that 'the *Logos* became flesh and lived among us'; and also because it introduces the final part of the Prologue where John's teaching about who and what Jesus is reaches its plain and amazing climax.

Verse 14 is stark – 'the *Logos* became flesh and lived among us'. I hope it is clear by now just what a mind-blowing statement that would have been for John's first readers. It is a claim made about Jesus of utterly staggering proportions. And yet it is not alone in the New Testament. A number of current New Testament scholars have said that the biggest question which historians of the Early Church and New Testament scholars need to work on is the question of how, within a couple of generations of his death, Christians were using amazingly exalted language about this crucified rabbi, healer and prophet. The titles of two of the books which explore this question sum it up very well: *How on earth did Jesus become a God?* (L Hurtado, Eerdmans, 2004) and *From Jewish Prophet to Gentile God* (M Casey, Westminster/John Knox, 1991). The exalted language used in the New Testament about Jesus is plain enough. It appears that one of the earliest creeds, if that's the right word, was the very short 'Jesus is Lord' (Romans 10.9, 2 Corinthians 4.5, Philippians 2.11), a very political and potentially very dangerous statement in a culture where Caesar was Lord, and a very radical statement for Jewish converts to make for whom 'Lord' was one of their most common words for God. Whether the New Testament itself actually reaches the point of calling Jesus 'God' is an open question, for the two key texts at Romans 9.5 and Titus 2.13 are ambiguous, but it is certainly moving in that direction. Revelation pictures him as exalted at God's right hand, and Thomas' words of commitment to the Risen Christ – 'my Lord and my God' – come close, but these two are among the latest parts of the New Testament to be written. It is also an open question in John's Prologue itself. Its opening verses say that the *Logos* was present in the beginning, say twice that the *Logos* was 'with' God and once that the *Logos* 'was' God, or possibly, 'was divine'. At the very least the

Prologue certainly wants to suggest an intimate connection of the *Logos* with God. Much the same is true of the amazing hymn in Colossians 1.15-20. Far earlier than all of these, however, is the famous hymn which Paul quotes in Philippians 2, which seems to have been in use at least by the AD 50s, as Paul quotes it in this letter written around AD 60. There is no doubt about the status given to Christ in this hymn:

> though he was in the form of God, (Christ) did not regard equality with God as something to be exploited, but emptied himself, taking the form of a slave, being born in human likeness. And being found in human form, he humbled himself and became obedient to the point of death –even death on a cross. Therefore God also highly exalted him and gave him the name that is above every name, so that at the name of Jesus every knee should bend, in heaven and on earth and under the earth, and every tongue should confess that Jesus Christ is Lord, to the glory of God the Father. (Philippians 2.6–11)

How and why the first Christians moved from believing in Jesus as prophet, rabbi, healer and even 'Messiah' to beliefs like this about him is the subject of much current writing; and this part of the Prologue is part of that discussion.

Before we move on there are two details in verse 14 which need a word of explanation. The verse says that the *Logos* 'became flesh', and it uses the Greek word *sarx*. Greek has two particular words for 'body', *sarx* and *soma*. The one tends to convey ideas about the body as weak and frail, even as rather nasty, while the other has no unpleasant overtones or nuances. You can see something of those overtones where the word is used in verse 13. The interesting thing is that it is that word *sarx* which is used again in verse 14. It is not that the *Logos* 'became a human being' (as in the Good News Bible – that would be a good translation if the other word had been used), but that the *Logos* became 'flesh' (as in all the other major translations). You can see more of the overtones of the word when you remember that old trio of nasties which traditionally make life tempting and tough for Christians – 'the world, the flesh and the Devil'. When the Bible was translated into Latin a word with similar overtones was used, from which we get the English word 'carnal', leading us to the word 'Incarnation' for the doctrine of God the Son becoming human. John is certainly at pains to make the point that the *Logos* became a real human being, not a shadow of one or some sort of semi-ethereal appearance of one – which is what one group of early Christians thought Jesus was – a god who lived among us but whose feet never got dirty, whose tummy never rumbled with hunger and who never really suffered, bled and died. Not so, insists John, Jesus was real! But is he hinting at more than that? Is he suggesting the complete identification of Jesus with us in our weakness and frailty? Even in our proneness to sin? 'Tempted in all points as we are, yet without sin' is how the letter to the Hebrews puts it (Hebrews 4.15), and the sinless of Jesus became orthodox teaching: but is John possibly suggesting by his use of *sarx* that Jesus was even more fully human than that?

The other interesting word here is the verb translated 'lived' in NRSV. The *New International Version* has 'lived for a while', *Revised English Bible* has 'made his home' and *Today's New International Version* has 'made his dwelling'. The verb means living in a tent, and the noun is the word used for the 'Tabernacle', the portable shrine which the Israelites carried with them as they journeyed in the wilderness after leaving Egypt and in which God 'dwelt among them' (Exodus 25.9). Later on various prophets longed for the time when God would 'dwell' with them again (Ezekiel 37.27, Joel 3.17, Zechariah 2.10). That time has now come, says John.

'Life', 'light', 'glory', 'grace' and 'truth'

Earlier on we identified these five words as other particularly important words in the Prologue and now we must explore them a little more.

Verse 3 describes the role of the *Logos* in giving life to all of creation. The *Logos* is with God in the beginning and 'all things came into being through him'. The *Logos* is the source of 'life'. Verse 10 repeats that the world came into being through the *Logos*. Verse 12 picks up this image of the *Logos* as life-giver and speaks of the new life which he now brings. This will be an important theme in the rest of the gospel of John. Jesus will teach much about 'eternal life', which is the life of a new age or new quality which begins now and continues beyond death. John teaches that the purpose of Jesus' own earthly life is to give people access to this new life (John 3.16). In the gospel Jesus teaches that this life is accessed by 'believing in' him (10.10 and also 3.36, 5.24, 6.40, 10.28, 14.6). The gospel ends with the note that helping people to come to the point of believing, and so finding 'life in his name' is the reason why John has written a gospel at all (20.31).

Verse 4 names the gift of life as the gift of light, 'light for all people' and light which darkness has failed to extinguish. Verse 9 repeats that this 'true light', which 'enlightens everyone', was coming into the world even as The Baptist was speaking of this light to come. This theme is repeated through the gospel, especially in terms of the conflict between the light and the darkness. The coming of the light creates a crisis, a 'judgement', which divides those who choose light from those who choose darkness (3.17–21, 12.35–36). Jesus is 'the light of the world' (8.12, 9.5, 12.46).

Verse 14 uses the term 'glory' for what is seen when the *Logos* is 'made flesh' and dwells among us, a very particular and extraordinary 'glory'. The supreme glory is that of God, and the word denotes his majesty, splendour, beauty, power and authority enjoyed and celebrated in the real world of heaven, and only occasionally glimpsed here, as by Moses on the mountain-top or in the Tent (Numbers 14.1) and in visions like those of Isaiah (Isaiah 6) or Ezekiel (Ezekiel 1-3). Jesus is, John claims, far more than a glimpse, and cites in the gospel a number of 'signs' where this glory is 'made manifest', clearly and plainly seen and disclosed, from the wedding at Cana (2.11), through the raising of Lazarus (11.4 and 40) to supremely in the cross (17.4–5). Claims to such glory are, however, controversial and disputed (7.14–18).

Verse 14 identifies 'grace' as a core component of this extraordinary 'glory', and verse 16 notes that we have received this grace in abundance. Verse 17 insists there is something new in this grace, better than even the best of blessings which God has given before. As modern Christians we need to be alert to the reference to Moses in verse 17. Almost from the beginning some Christians contrasted their wonderful experience of God's love in Jesus with what they called the dead, old, legalistic religion of Judaism; or their new 'Gospel' with the old 'Law'; or even the Nice God of the New Testament with the Nasty God of the Old. Given this long history of caricaturing Judaism and of making vastly superior claims for Christianity, it is easy to read verse 17 as saying that the new experience we have received in Jesus Christ is infinitely better than what was offered previously in the old and inadequate Law given through and represented by Moses. I suggest that that misreads verse 17. Importantly it gets the Old Testament sense of 'Law' (*Torah*) wrong: it is not a set of burdensome laws to keep in the hope of securing God's approval – the familiar Christian caricature – but God's teaching and guidance given to his people as a blessing to help them live life to the full. In the light of that I suggest that it makes better sense if this verse is understood as saying that great though the blessings were which God gave through his wonderful life-giving guidance and teaching through Moses, what he gives now in Jesus is even better. Unlike 'life' and 'light', the word 'grace' only occurs in these verses in this gospel. It sums up the Old Testament's core teaching about God as 'merciful and gracious, slow to anger and abounding in steadfast love' (Exodus 34.6–7, Psalm 103 etc. which I explore in *Let us bless the Lord*, Inspire, 2006). Jesus, the Prologue claims, embodies God's amazing generosity and kindness.

Verse 9 identifies the one to whom John testifies as the 'true' light. Verse 14 identifies 'truth' as the second core component of 'glory'. Verse 17 insists there is something new in this truth, above and beyond the great truths already made known. One of the key 'I am' sayings which John puts on the lips of Jesus is 'I am the way, the truth, and the life' (John 14.6). Coming to a knowledge of this truth, and finding this way of relating to God is liberating (8.32) and the promise is that after Jesus is taken away this journey into truth will continue (16.13).

Obviously, to explore these important words further will take us too far away from where we need to be. All that needs to be said here is that these 'big' words need to be attached to the meaning of *Logos* if we are to build up any kind of picture of what John is saying about Jesus at the beginning of his gospel.

'God's only Son' or 'God the only Son'?

And then there is verse 18, and this verse too must be considered. All translations agree that the opening and closing of the verse are straightforward enough. It opens with a statement that no one has ever seen God; and it closes with a statement that one who is close to the Father's heart has made him known. That 'one' is Jesus, and 'making God known' is what Jesus is all about, so the Prologue concludes.

However, between the opening and closing statements of this verse lies a tricky translation problem.

The NRSV translation is: 'No one has ever seen God. *It is God the only Son*, who is close to the Father's heart, who has made him known'. For those words in italics the old *Authorised Version* has 'the only begotten Son'; *Revised English Bible* has 'God's only Son'; *New International Version* has 'God the only Son'; *New Jerusalem Bible* has 'It is the only Son' and, paraphrasing it more, *Good News Bible* has 'the only Son, who is the same as God' while *Today's New International Version* has 'but the one and only [Son] who is himself God'. Most of them offer alternatives or explanations in footnotes. The differences are all to do with ancient manuscripts and three words: *monogenes*, God and Son. Complication number one is that *monogenes* can be translated as 'only-begotten' or 'beloved' or, best of all, 'unique,' or as 'only-begotten/unique son'. Complication number two is that some of the ancient manuscripts have *monogenes* + Son and others have *monogenes* + God. A useful rule in sorting this kind of thing out is to see which reading is harder, and then rule out the others, on the ground that a copyist faced with a reading he found difficult or impossible to understand was seriously tempted to simplify it and make it make sense. On those grounds scholars suggest that *monogenes* + Son (which gives us 'the only begotten Son' of the *Authorised Version*) is not the original one. That leaves *monogenes* + God, which ought to be translated as 'the unique God', and if that is correct, then this is another verse in the New Testament which explicitly calls Jesus God, to be added to the two we mentioned earlier. Complication number three is that the phrase *monogenes* + Son is found nearby in John at 3.16 and *monogenes* + Son + God at 3.18. Make of this what you will, I am not sure either! I will point out, however, that one of John's favourite ways of speaking about Jesus is as the 'Son', and that he does so not in the sense that the Messiah was the adopted 'Son of God', which we saw in the Old Testament and in Matthew and Luke, but in a different sense entirely that, for good or ill, later Christian theologians would develop into the doctrine of the Trinity. Whatever else verse 18 might mean, it says that when we see Jesus we are seeing God, that, as it were, in Jesus we see right into the heart of God – a challenging point repeated in different ways in 'the Father and I are one' in John 10.30 and 'Whoever has seen me has seen the Father' in John 14.9.

The two subsidiary themes

We noted earlier that there were two subsidiary themes in the Prologue, one about John the Baptist in verses 6–8 and verse 15 and the other about the response to Jesus in verses 9–13. It is only in these verses that John's story of the birth of Jesus, if we can call it that, comes anywhere near to those of Matthew and Luke. John's interlacing of material about John the Baptist in the Prologue is reminiscent of Luke who weaves the stories of their births together, and all three gospels move from birth story or Prologue to tell of John the Baptist and his preaching ministry, and then of Jesus' baptism by John in the Jordan river. Then, in John's second subsidiary theme, we see something of the pain and foreboding found in Matthew's birth story, that the life of Jesus is a story of rejection by his own people, represented in Matthew by Herod and the leaders in Jerusalem, and of good news and hope in an opening out of the good news to others. The tension in verses 10–13 will be present throughout John's gospel, which contains some of the sharpest words against 'the Jews' in the New Testament.

The birth of Jesus in John and what this tells us about him

At the beginning of this chapter I invited you to complete this sentence, 'According to John, this Jesus who was born of Mary is . . .' Now I would like you to look at what you wrote then, and see if you would like to change it in any way in the light of what you have read since, without reading on beyond the end of this sentence.

Now I invite you to compare your first sentence with two of mine: 'According to John, this Jesus who was born of Mary is the embodiment of God's eternal plan, purpose and power', and 'According to John, this Jesus who was born of Mary is the human expression of God.'

I think it is clear that John starts from somewhere rather different from Matthew and Luke. He writes like a philosopher, reminding his readers of what they had learned in school about the *Logos*, and then moving on to say that Jesus is nothing less than the *Logos* Incarnate. I think I made it clear that I get rather annoyed that our Bibles make that major point very difficult to understand by translating *Logos* as 'Word'. This all adds up to a significantly different answer to our question than that given by

Matthew or Luke. The birth stories in Matthew and Luke offer us, in different ways, an introduction to the story of Jesus the Messiah. John, in his Prologue, offers us an introduction to the story of Jesus the Cosmic Presence, if I may introduce a new phrase at this late stage of the book.

Postscript on the Gospel of John

Anyone who reads the four gospels in the New Testament can't help but notice that very Matthew, Mark and Luke are similar in very many ways, and occasionally they are identical, so much so that scholars call them the 'Synoptic' gospels, as they have the same outlook and perspective. Once you get past the birth stories, their treatment of the actual ministry of Jesus is very similar. Jesus lives and works in Galilee, and only goes to Jerusalem for the visit that results in his crucifixion. Jesus teaches about 'the kingdom of God' and much of his teaching is done in short sharp sentences and in parables. By contrast John begins with a prologue rather than with stories, and his story of the ministry of Jesus has a different shape; here Jesus is frequently found travelling between Galilee and Jerusalem. In John the teaching of Jesus is different too: no parables and instead long, complicated discourses which don't mention the 'kingdom of God' but do focus almost exclusively on who Jesus is. In the first three gospels Jesus is remarkably reticent about saying anything about himself; in the fourth he never stops talking about himself. All of this has led scholars to work on the question of whether John or the Synoptics give us a better picture of Jesus as he actually was, and a better idea of what he actually taught. Majority opinion favours the Synoptics and has always favoured them since the scholarly debate began in earnest in the eighteenth century.

Long before that, however, the Early Fathers were also aware that John and the other three were different, and the great second-century scholar and teacher Clement (AD c.150-215), who headed the famous Christian Bible School in Alexandria in Egypt, is usually credited with calling John 'the Spiritual Gospel' to mark out its distinctiveness. He wrote,

> 'Last of all John, perceiving that the external facts had been made plain in the Gospels, being urged by his friends and inspired by the Spirit, composed a spiritual gospel.'

The conclusion I personally draw from the scholarly debate, and helped by this huge hint from Clement of Alexandria, is to think of the Fourth gospel as the aged John's reflection on what Jesus means to him and who Jesus is for him. If I want to know what Jesus said and did I turn to Matthew, Mark and Luke, although there too I bear in mind that none of them gives a photograph of Jesus, a diary of his doings nor a verbatim account of his teaching; instead each paints a portrait and has their own agenda in what they write and how they write it. Even in those three it's hard to get back behind the 'Christ of faith' to the 'Jesus of history', to use rather loaded terms. With John it is harder still. What we do have, in John, it seems to me is essentially a set of reflections on the significance of Jesus for this old teacher and, no doubt, for his community. So all those well-loved sayings that we find on the lips of Jesus in the Fourth gospel such as 'I am the Bread of Life, 'I am the Light of the World' and 'I am the Way, the Truth and the Life' are not, for me, sayings of Jesus about himself. Instead they are sayings about Jesus from John, which speak of the way in which, through a long life of faithfulness, he has found Jesus to be 'the True Vine', 'the Resurrection and the Life' and 'the Good Shepherd' and so on. In other words, here is testimony to the significance of Jesus from one early Christian and his church which invites us to faith in that same Jesus in our own time and situation. And it is testimony, of course, that begins in the Prologue itself.

Questions for reflection

1   What do you think of my translations which read 'Idea' or 'Energy' instead of 'Word' for Logos? Or are you happy with 'Word'?

2   We have looked quite carefully at John's Prologue. Has anything I have said about it disturbed you? Has anything excited you?

3   What do you think of my two sentences about John? Which do you prefer? Why?

4   What do you make of the differences between John and the Other Three, and of my approach to John's material?

Conclusion

We have looked carefully and seriously at the birth stories in Matthew and Luke and at the Prologue to the gospel of John. We have seen that in answer to the question 'Who is this Jesus who was born of Mary?' Matthew and Luke give a similar answer, that he is the 'Messiah', though their stories are quite different. We have seen that John gives a very different answer, that he is the 'Logos embodied'.

In 1985 Jaroslav Pelikan wrote an influential book called *Jesus through the Centuries* which looked at the many and varied ways in which Jesus has been understood in different cultures and communities over the past two millennia. An illustrated version was published in the 1990s. In 2000 the National Gallery held a major and hugely popular exhibition of paintings of Christ called *Seeing Salvation*, showing how Christ has been depicted in art through the centuries. The catalogue of the exhibition was published as *The Image of Christ*. In the 1990s the Church Missionary Society, USPG and the Methodist Church jointly published a set of postcards, activity sheets and OHP slides called *The Christ we Share* containing 30 images of Christ, most of them contemporary, from around the world. All these show how different writers and artists, from the beginning of Christianity to the present day, have seen something significant in Jesus and have struggled to express the significance he has for them in different ways, using varying words, ideas and images. Hymn-writers ancient and modern and contemporary writers of worship songs do the same. That process begins in the New Testament itself where over 40 different names or titles are given to Jesus.

In this little book we have looked at what the opening pages of the gospels say about Jesus. We have seen that each in their own way gives testimony to Jesus as they understand him, and that they understand him rather differently. We have seen that each is trying to explain the significance that Jesus has for them. Which is why this book is called 'Who *is* this Jesus who was born of Mary?' and not 'Who *was* . . .?'

That difference matters. And it invites each one of us to think about what Jesus means to us, and how we can express the enormous significance he has for us in our very different world and culture today.

Postscript 1: Christmas – the facts and the fantasies

Just in case any of you are thinking that some of this is radical stuff that you have never heard before, or in case you want a summary of my argument in this little book, here is how I put it in an article in the *Western Morning News* on December 23rd, 2000, when I was Chair of the Cornwall District of the Methodist Church (reproduced by kind permission of the editor).

*****

Hard facts about the first Christmas are few. Jesus was born. His mother was Mary. That's about it. We don't know when, where or anything about the circumstances surrounding the birth. That might worry some people, but it needn't. It obviously didn't worry the first Christian thinker, Paul; or the first Gospel writer, Mark, for that's all they said on the subject. Twenty years later it was different. Then, Matthew and Luke began their biographies of Jesus with stories about his birth. Later still, John began his meditation on the life and meaning of Jesus with some popular philosophy.

Christmas in Christian churches today tends to major on the two stories in Matthew and Luke. Occasionally we then get hung up on the "Is it true?" and the "Did it really happen?" sort of questions, even though asking those kinds of questions about much in the Bible never actually gets us very far. More often, sadly, we don't ask any questions at all. I want to look at two much better questions: 'Why did they tell such stories in the first place?' and 'What do these stories mean?'

The answer to the first question is that the Christmas stories were a celebration. In story, drama, poetry and song the first Christians celebrated the impact Jesus of Nazareth had on them, on how they thought, on their values and attitudes and on their lifestyles. They didn't at that stage produce creeds or work out definitions. Instead they sang songs and told stories because that was the way their Jewish culture traditionally expressed its deepest convictions about the meaning of life. Today, Christians still use those old stories and sing those old songs in nativity plays, carol services and on Christmas cards to celebrate what Jesus means to them.

The answer to the second question is harder, because something has happened to the two stories. They have been merged into one and additions made. If you disentangle them you find that Matthew and Luke tell different stories and the differences between them cannot be reconciled. Both are giving their testimony to Jesus. For Matthew he is the great New Teacher, whose teaching is for all people everywhere. For Luke he is the humane and compassionate 'Friend of Sinners', companion of ordinary people and outcasts, the great humanitarian.

Matthew tells a dark and tragic story. Jesus is the Messiah God has promised. But it all goes wrong. The baby is born at home in Bethlehem. Wise men arrive, having asked Herod the way. He attempts to kill the baby. Joseph and Mary flee to Egypt as refugees. Thus the Messiah is born but his own people do not accept him. Foreign wise men worship him but Herod and the wise men of Jerusalem reject him.

Luke's birth story is homely. Jesus' cousin, John the Baptist, is born to an infertile couple, a sure sign that God is at work. The angel Gabriel appears to Mary, who lives in Nazareth, announces her own pregnancy. Mary and Joseph journey to Bethlehem for a Roman census and Jesus is born in a stable there. Shepherds visit. All the people in Luke's story are ordinary; none are rich, powerful or important.

One of these stories will probably appeal more than the other, for each Christian sees Jesus in their own way, but neither will displace the Combined Version celebrated annually in churches. Bethlehem. A stable. The baby in a manger. Mary sits. Joseph stands. Shepherds kneel. Three kings offer gifts. Ox and ass look on. A star. Angels. Most of that picture comes from Matthew and Luke. Now add the music, and more appears each year. Winter's snow. Three ships. Merry gentlemen. None of this comes from the Bible and none of these things ever happened, of course, but we sing old carols and write new ones because in imagination, fantasy and poetry they speak to us of things that really matter.

The poets and singers who give us these gifts continue what Matthew and Luke began. They give us stories, images, pictures, songs and words with which to make sense of life. Then, if we choose to do so we can decide to live out these particular stories, and to sing these particular songs which celebrate Jesus of Nazareth as God's greatest gift to humanity.

Postscript 2: On the carol 'Cradled in a manger, meanly ...'

This appeared as chapter 3 in my little book *Desert Island Hymns Faith which Sings with Heart and Mind* (Southleigh Publications 1996). In that book I looked at the eight hymns which for me sum up the heart of the Christian Faith. The book is out of print now but available from Kindle or as a free download from www.stephendawes.com.

Cradled in a manger, meanly

Cradled in a manger, meanly
Laid the Son of Man His head;
Sleeping His first earthly slumber
Where the oxen had been fed.
Happy were those shepherds listening
To the holy angel's word;
Happy they within that stable,
Worshipping their infant Lord.

Happy all who hear the message
Of His coming from above;
Happier still who hail His coming,
And with praises greet His love.
Blessed Saviour, Christ most holy,
In a manger Thou didst rest;
Canst Thou stoop again, yet lower,
And abide within my breast?

Evil things are there before Thee;
In the heart, where they have fed,
Wilt thou pitifully enter,
Son of Man, and lay Thy head?
Enter, then, O Christ most holy;
Make a Christmas in my heart;
Make a heaven of my manger:
It is heaven where Thou art.

And to those who never listened
To the message of Thy birth,
Who have winter, but no Christmas
Bringing them Thy peace on earth,
Send to these the joyful tidings;
By all people, in each home,
Be there heard the Christmas anthem:
Praise to God, the Christ has come!

This is a favourite Methodist carol, written by a Methodist minister, George Stringer Rowe (1830-1913) for the children's magazine *At Home and Abroad* and then published in the Methodist Sunday-School Hymnbook of 1879. It is no.98 in *Hymns and Psalms*. I love this carol for many reasons, but I have chosen it as one of my desert island hymns for three particular ones. First, because of the powerful climax of the last verse, 'Praise to God, the Christ has come!' which for me sounds the right note not only for Christmas but for every day. Second, because it is firmly based on one of the two different Christmas stories in the New Testament, the one told in Luke's gospel. Third, because it talks about the coming of Christ into our lives today, not simply about his coming a long time ago in a place far away.

If we ask, 'What are the hard facts about Christmas?' then the answer is very brief. All that we know for certain is that Jesus was born, and that his mother's name was Mary. We cannot put a date on his birth to a year, let alone to a day. Neither can we be sure where he was born nor about the circumstances surrounding his birth. But asking that question about anything in the Bible never gets you very far, and though some people want to keep on asking it, it is not a very important question. A much more important question to ask about the Bible is, What do these stories mean? Another important one is, Why did they tell such stories in the first place? If you ask those sorts of questions about the Christmas stories you really can get somewhere.

So what about the Christmas stories we tell each year in nativity plays and carol services, in cribs and on Christmas cards? In these stories we are celebrating the heart of our faith. In them we are saying, Praise to God, the Christ has come! In story, drama, poetry and music we are thanking God for his gift to us of Jesus. In the great festival of Christmas we are using old stories and sometimes new ones to say what Jesus means to us. In celebrating him in this way and telling these stories we are not talking about what happened when he was born, but about something much more important. We are saying what his birth among us meant and means! Which is exactly what Matthew and Luke were doing when they told their different Christmas stories at the beginning of their gospels.

We are all familiar with the Christmas Story as it is told in church and chapel in crib and nativity play and pictured on Christmas cards. There is the baby lying in a manger. Mary and Joseph look on, sharing the stable with ox and ass. Shepherds kneel to worship. Three kings or wise men offer their gifts. Over all is the star which guided them, and angels too. Most of that picture, though not all of it, comes from the two stories in Matthew and Luke. Other carols let their imagination fly free and in addition to talking about oxen and asses, which are one of the features which don't appear anywhere in the Bible stories at all, also sing about the kings sailing into Bethlehem in three ships, sometime past three-o-clock, amidst the winter's snow, to see a baby who never cries, while all the bells in heaven are ringing in joy at the event. These carols are doing just what Matthew and Luke did, they are trying to show what the birth of Jesus means! So letting imaginations run riot, they encourage us to join the celebration, for those who have discovered the joy of Christmas have so much to celebrate because, 'Praise to God, the Christ has come!'

One of the things that we don't do at Christmas, and it's a pity, is to look carefully at what Matthew or Luke say in their own stories, and to look at what is said in other parts of the New Testament about the birth of Jesus. When you do this and look carefully at what the Bible says about Christmas you see that the full-scale nativity play, for instance, is not there. In that play parts of the Christmas story from Matthew are used together with parts from Luke: but other bits of both are left out, because that's the only way that two different and at times conflicting stories can be harmonised. So before we get to the carol let us have a quick look at what the New Testament says about Christmas.

The earliest gospel of the four is Mark, and it doesn't mention the birth of Jesus at all. The earliest Christmas reference in the New Testament is St Paul's statement, 'when the fullness of time had come, God sent his Son, born of a woman, born ...' (Galatians 4.4). Another early one is in the hymn he quotes in Philippians 2.6-8, that Jesus Christ,

> 'though he was in the form of God, did not regard equality with God as something to be exploited, but emptied himself, taking the form of a slave, being born in human likeness. And being found in human form, he humbled himself ...'

Both of these make the same point as the later reference in 1 John 4.2 that you can tell true spirits from false because the true ones 'confess that Jesus Christ has come in the flesh'. These are important glimpses of the Christmas faith of the early Christians because they are all asides. In these passages the writers are really discussing something else and mention the birth of Jesus only as an illustration to make a different point. But each of them stress that Jesus was born and that he was a real human being. In stressing that, they all counter a very real threat that was coming into the early church from a group of people who did not believe that God or God's spirit could possibly become human. Spirit was spirit, and spirit was good; flesh was flesh, and flesh was bad. These folk believed that in human beings spirit, or soul, was imprisoned in a human body, and that was bad enough: but God's spirit could never be contaminated like that. At the most some talked about the man, Jesus of Nazareth, in whom God's spirit came to dwell at his baptism and departed at the crucifixion. This was too much for others who would not believe that Jesus was a real person at all. The New Testament will have none of that. It insists that the Lord of the Church was a real human being who ate and drank, laughed and cried, got angry and weary, was born and died.

Three of the four gospels begin with Christmas theology: Matthew and Luke give us their belief about Jesus by painting pictures and John gives his by straight teaching.

John begins his gospel with a paragraph which would have been easy for all his first readers to understand. Yet for us his 'In the beginning was the Word', which we hear every Christmas, goes right over our heads. When he wrote, 'In the beginning was the *Logos*, and the *Logos* was ...' all his first readers would have simply nodded their heads and wondered when he was going to get to the point. Greek readers would have known that the *Logos* (we can translate the term as word, speech, reason, idea, rationality, reason and a number of other things besides) was the principle which held everything together, the idea behind all life, the meaning and ground of it all; and so these readers would simply nod agreement to what John had written. The world was no accident, there was intelligence, meaning and purpose behind it. Jewish readers would have immediately thought of Genesis 1 and all the ways in which 'God spoke and all things came to be'. They too would have understood what John was saying and agreed with it. It was God's idea that was behind creation, and his powerful word that called it into being. The first four verses of John 1 would have been almost stating the obvious to those first readers, whereas for us translating *Logos* as 'Word' makes no sense at all. But both of those groups of early readers would have been jerked upright by verse 14, 'The *Logos* became flesh'. That would have shocked and amazed them all, and for John that is where the good news of Jesus begins. Unfortunately, by the time we get to verse 14 the congregation has switched off, which is a pity because look at what it says about Jesus, that 'the divine idea behind the universe - the meaning and energy of life itself - has become flesh, and Jesus is his name'.

Matthew's gospel begins with a genealogy which is meaningless to us but crucial to Matthew's point and, he would have hoped, convincing to his fellow Jews. It traces the lineage of Abraham, the father of all the Jewish people, down to great King David and then down to Jesus. It is done to prove that Jesus 'who is called the Messiah' (1.16) is in fact 'the Messiah, the son of David, the son of Abraham' (1.1). It is done to show that Jesus is the 'long-expected' one, 'born to set his people free', as an Advent hymn puts it. Then Matthew tells his story about how this Jesus the Messiah was born. The story is set in the time when Herod is King of Judea (he died in 4 BC). An angel appears to Joseph to tell him that his fiancée is pregnant and that this pregnancy is the work of God. Joseph still married her and the baby was born at home in Bethlehem. Wise men followed a star and brought gifts but asked Herod the way. He looked for the baby for different reasons and when he couldn't find him killed all the young boys in the area. Meanwhile Joseph and Mary had fled with the baby to Egypt as refugees. They stayed there until Herod died and then they tried to go home to Bethlehem. Finding a son of Herod on the throne they decided to go to Galilee, a separate country, and settled in the village of Nazareth instead. All through this story Matthew quotes Old Testament texts to show that in all of this God is at work to save his people, but it is a painfully sad story. The Messiah is born but 'he came to his own people, and his own people did not accept him'. That is how John puts it in a plain sentence in John 1.11 but Matthew puts it in a story form. Jesus is worshipped by foreign wise men, priests of an eastern religion, but rejected by Herod and the wise men and priests of Jerusalem. The story of Jesus' life will unfold in the same way, and Matthew will end his gospel with this Jesus telling his disciples to 'go out into all the world' (28.19).

Luke's birth story is very different. It starts with the birth of Jesus' relative, John the Baptist, to very aged parents. God is at work in such births, remember the birth of Isaac to Abraham and Sarah? The angel Gabriel appears to Mary who lives in Nazareth, announces her own imminent pregnancy and tells her about Elizabeth's. She visits her. Mary and Joseph become engaged, and they have to journey to Bethlehem for a census. There the baby is born in a stable because there is no room in the inn. Shepherds visit. After eight days the baby is circumcised and four weeks later they take him to the Temple in Jerusalem where they offer the proper thanksgiving. After all that they go home to Nazareth. All through this story there are songs of praise to God for what he is doing in all of this. This child is the 'Son of the Most High' (1.32), the 'Son of David and King of the Jews' (1.33), 'Saviour, Messiah and Lord' (2.11). All the people involved in Luke's story are ordinary, none are rich, powerful or important. That is the way Jesus' life will unfold. In Luke he will live among such people and care especially for the despised and the outcast. Luke also has a genealogy but doesn't give it until the end of chapter 3; and in it he traces Jesus back past David and Abraham to Adam. He makes the same point there. Jesus is for all humanity.

John begins his gospel with theology - after all John 1.1-18 is hard to understand so it must be theology - and Matthew and Luke do the same! In their stories they are expressing their faith in Jesus, and that faith is every bit as rich in theology as John's. Their birth stories do not actually tell us any more of the facts of Jesus' birth than John's opening statements, but in all kinds of ways they illustrate who Jesus is. In a sense their stories are much more like obituaries which sum up the meaning of a person's life than birth certificates which contain the facts of a baby's birth. George Stringer Rowe recognises that, and what he does in his beautiful carol is, beginning with Luke's story, to go on to point out the significance of Jesus for us today, so that there may be a Christmas in our hearts.

> Cradled in a manger, meanly / Laid the Son of Man His head;
> Sleeping His first earthly slumber / Where the oxen had been fed.
> Happy were those shepherds listening / To the holy angel's word;
> Happy they within that stable / Worshipping their infant Lord.

'Meanly' picks up one of the key themes in Luke's gospel. In his birth stories Elizabeth and Zechariah, Mary and Joseph, the shepherds, Simeon and Anna are all 'little' people, nobodies from nowhere in particular. The baby is born in a stable, wrapped in poor 'swaddling cloths' and put in a manger. Life goes on its way and his birth is unnoticed by the world at large. And that is the way, according to Luke, that Jesus grew up and lived. He made his friends among ordinary people and he cared for life's nobodies, like the poor, women, lepers and outcasts even though some of those outcasts were rich ones like Zachaeus the tax-collector. The first people to thank God for Jesus were shepherds, rough, somewhat despised, not very religious, certainly very ordinary people.

The story of the shepherds in Luke 2.8-20 is a brilliant piece of story-telling. Imagine yourself on that hillside. An angel appears with a message, a message that gets more wonderful with each word. After the shock the words begin to sink in - for you ... good news ... great joy ... today ... in David's city ... a Saviour ... Christ ... the Lord. By this time you are agog with excitement. The crescendo rises to its climax, This will be your sign ... Then in verse 12 the anti-climax which is the key to Luke's whole gospel story of Jesus, and it doesn't need much imagination to feel the disappointment and the let-down - a baby, swaddling cloths, a manger. Some saviour! Some Lord! Some hope! You must be joking! But they decide to give it a try, and they find that indeed in that stable is their true happiness.

Happy is the other key word of this verse and it is carried over into the next. It is a quiet and simple happiness, unsought-for, found in an unexpected place.

> Happy all who hear the message / Of His coming from above;
> Happier still who hail His coming / And with praises greet His love.
> Blessed Saviour, Christ most holy / In a manger Thou didst rest;

Canst Thou stoop again, yet lower / And abide within my breast?

This verse links the manger and our contemporary world. It begins with the happiness of Christmas shared by all who enjoy the Festive Season, and especially by those who not only know the Christmas Story but also respond to it. The hymn says that there is nothing wrong with this sort of happiness, or with festivity and fun. It goes further. It says that the more you centre your celebrations on Jesus, 'the reason for the season' as the car sticker puts it, the happier you will be.

There is a change in the second half of the verse and from then on the carol draws our attention away from the shepherds and their manger to us and ours. The significance of Christmas can only be known when there is a Christmas in our hearts. As the significance of Jesus was only discovered by people in Galilee and Jerusalem when they listened to him, took him seriously, believed him and committed themselves to him, so for us Christmas only becomes significant when it ceases to be a celebration of a dim and distant event long ago and becomes something that speaks to us of the love of God and the life of God present in our lives, our communities and our world today. From here on the hymn becomes a prayer to Christ to stoop again, yet lower, and abide within my breast.

Note the titles used for Christ in this hymn: Blessed Saviour, Christ most holy and Son of Man. 'Son of Man' is used very often in the gospels and rarely in the rest of the New Testament. Jesus calls himself, 'The Son of Man' in what is probably no more than the Aramaic equivalent of the posher English 'one' instead of 'I'. The hymn uses it as a title in both verse 1 and verse 3, and in both place it speaks of the humility of Jesus. As he was put in a manger as a baby, so now he is willing to come into our equally grubby hearts. In verses 2 and 3 our Lord is called 'Christ most holy'. Though we tend to use 'Christ' as if it was Jesus' surname it began life as a title. It was the Greek word for the Hebrew term, 'Messiah', the title of God's anointed kings of old and the title for the one they hoped God would soon send to make Israel great again. The New Testament believes that Jesus was that long-awaited Messiah, though his new kingdom turned out to be very different from the one that was expected. In the hymn the word is still used as a proper title, 'Christ most holy'. The angels also were called holy in verse 1. In the Bible to say that God is holy is to acknowledge his power and majesty, his love and his awesome purity. It is put perfectly in the third verse of Reginald Heber's hymn, 'Holy, holy, holy, Lord God Almighty',

Only Thou art holy, there is none beside Thee,
perfect in power, in love and purity.

So when the hymn talks about 'Christ most holy' in the same breath as it talks about him in Bethlehem's manger or the manger of our hearts, it expresses something of the amazing mystery which is at the heart of the Christian Faith. That, somehow, Jesus is 'God with us'. This is put poetically, for how else can it be put, nowhere better than in these words from Charles Wesley's usually unsung great Christmas hymn, 'Glory be to God on high',

God the invisible appears / God, the blest, the great I AM,
Sojourns in this vale of tears / And Jesus is His name.

Him the angels all adored / Their Maker and their King;
Tidings of their humbled Lord / They now to mortals bring.
Emptied of His majesty / Of His dazzling glories shorn,
Being's source begins to be / And God himself is born.

That was the hymn I nearly chose for my Christmas desert island hymn selection, but as I'm always getting into trouble for choosing carols nobody knows I thought better of it. The third title, 'Blessed Saviour', I will leave to the chapter after next.

Evil things are there before Thee / In the heart, where they have fed,
Wilt thou pitifully enter / Son of Man, and lay Thy head?
Enter, then, O Christ most holy / Make a Christmas in my heart;
Make a heaven of my manger / It is heaven where Thou art.

Verse 2 hinted that Christ's coming into our hearts involves stooping even lower than the manger, and verse 3 begins by recognising the nasty side of human life. There are evil things deep within us, alive, fed and nurtured by our wrongdoing and badness. The hymn recognises that but doesn't go on about it. There is a tendency for the church to go overboard when it comes to 'sin' and to paint a very gloomy picture of human beings as conceived and born in sin, totally unable to do anything good and to be on the road to eternal death simply as a result of being born that way. Traditional evangelism works on the assumption that if a person is to be 'saved' they must first of all recognise their sin and repent of it. In the same way very near the beginning of most services of worship come the prayers of confession. Now no one can dispute that human beings can and do foul up their own lives and the lives of others, nor that the life of our planet is seriously spoiled and marred by the attitudes and actions of its human inhabitants. There is plenty of evidence all around us that humanity is selfish and that its selfishness is deadly, and when we compare ourselves with either the holiness of God or with what we ourselves could be, then we have to admit that we look pretty shabby. This hymn recognises that but doesn't go on about it. It invites Christ to enter into our shabbiness, just as he entered into the shabbiness of the manger in the story. It also recognises that such love coming into our lives will transform them.

> And to those who never listened / To the message of Thy birth,
> Who have winter, but no Christmas / Bringing them Thy peace on earth,
> Send to these the joyful tidings / By all people, in each home,
> Be there heard the Christmas anthem:
> Praise to God, the Christ has come!

The hymn ends with a commission. There are those who have winter but no Christmas and the hymn ends on a note of concern for them. It wants them to hear the joyful tidings of the Christmas anthem so that the deadness of winter without the joy of the festivity in the middle of it, is replaced by heaven. There are, of course, people who are perfectly happy to have winter but no Christmas and Christians should be careful about assuming that theirs is not a happy lot. It is not necessarily the case that life without faith is dry, dreary and empty, or that life with faith is bright, happy and fulfilling. But the hymn ends on the positive note that the message about the love of God told in the Christmas story is a message worth telling and worth hearing. Words and tune (it must be *St Winifred*) combine for the climax of the last two lines. We celebrate and sing that there is joy for those who listen to the angels and do what the shepherds did. It insists that there is a Christmas anthem whose words and music are earthed in the historical fact that a baby was born to Mary and in the fact that the Christ who came to us at Bethlehem comes to us now, whoever we are, as we are and where we are. Its title expresses its theme,

> Praise to God, the Christ has come!